403(b)s

TSAs,

&

TDAs

A Guide for Teachers, Hospital Workers, and Non-Profit Employees

by John T. Hyland, CFA

BANTRY PRESS

BANTRY PRESS
OAKLAND, CALIFORNIA
1-800-797-5702

ISBN 0-9653248-1-8

RETAIL PRICE $12.95

TABLE OF CONTENTS

CHAPTER ONE

THE BEST RETIREMENT PLAN AROUND

If you are a teacher, a nurse, a college professor, or an employee of a charity, the chances are that you are covered by a type of retirement plan known as a 403(b). You may have heard this plan also referred to as a "TSA" or a "TDA". It does not matter; they are all the same thing.

The 403(b) retirement plan world is a large one. Over 250 billion dollars is invested by millions of active and retired workers in these plans. It is one of the oldest and most used retirement plans in the United States. If you don't have such a plan, chances are someone you know does. After all, who doesn't know at least one educator or hospital worker?

The good news is this is a valuable employee benefit. It may be the key to having a comfortable, financially secure retirement when you stop working. For those who start young, or who save aggressively, this plan can leave you quite well off at your retirement. For example, a 35 year old teacher who is willing to give up $50 a week in spending money could use their 403(b) plan to turn that into over $500,000 by retirement. Sound unrealistic?

For this quick example, we assume that they invest $67 a week pre-tax into their 403(b) via payroll deduction. That works out to about $50 less in their after-tax paycheck. We also assume that every five years they slightly increase their contribution to reflect increases in their salary (10% increase every 5 years, or 2% a year). The estimated rate of return on the 403(b) is 10% a year, which is a realistic long-term return. Finally, we assume that the teacher retires at age 62. If you save more each year, start sooner, or invest more aggressively, your results could be much higher.

Even for those getting a late start, using a 403(b) can make a difference to you at retirement. An extra $100,000 when you stop working can make a big difference in your lifestyle. It can be the difference between getting by and being comfortable. To reach that goal, a 50-year-old would need to save about $83 a week, given the same assumptions used above.

The 403(b) is often compared to its better known cousin, the 401(k) plan. In reality, the 403(b) is a superior plan. It may even come as a surprise to you that it has been around a lot longer than its' well-known

1

relative.

There are, however, two problems with this type of plan. The first is that reliable, objective information about these plans is definitely lacking. You can walk into almost any large bookstore and walk out with an armful of books about retirement plans and financial planning. Unfortunately, all of those books will tell you virtually nothing about your 403(b) plan. Usually what they say takes the form of a brief sentence or paragraph in which they breezily inform you that it is "very similar to a 401(k)". There is one problem with that statement; it is untrue.

The fact is there are several major differences between the 403(b) and the 401(k). The amount you can contribute annually is very different. Thus, a 403(b) may allow you to save more in taxes and for your retirement. Your choices of investment options are different. The role of your employer versus the role of a 401(k) employer is vastly different. Finally you have certain valuable options available to you that the 401(k) user lacks. No, it is not true that a 403(b) is just like a 401(k). In many respects, the 403(b) is a far better plan. Because of the special quirks of the 403(b) plan, a knowledgeable user can get great benefits out of it. This book will help you become a knowledgeable 403(b) user.

The second problem is that the employers in a 403(b) situation often do a poor job on behalf of their employees. The school districts, hospitals, colleges, etc. frequently do not give their employees a good set of investment options to use within their 403(b). An employee may find themselves with a 403(b) plan that is overly expensive, or gives a limited selection of options from which to choose. Sometimes this is because the employers do not feel that this is a major priority. Sometimes this is because they don't know any better. Like their employees, they often lack a clear understanding of the features and benefits of the 403(b), and they don't know how to shop around.

Too often, employers rely on the advice and guidance of the salesmen for life insurance companies and mutual funds who want them to use their products. Not surprisingly, these products often generate large profits and commissions for the life insurance companies and their agents. The result is that the employee ends up paying for the ignorance of the employer. This book will help the employees educate their employers as to what the plans are really about, and what choices are available. Finally, it will explain the escape hatch that an employee has if they are stuck with an unresponsive employer.

This book is will explain a number of things. They include:

WHAT A 403(b) PLAN IS. The history of the plans, what they are, and who is eligible.

HOW THEY WORK. Most 403(b) plan are set up the same. Here is a step-by-step guide to those arrangements.

WHY THEY ARE SO VALUABLE TO YOU. The major issue here is the value of tax deferral to your retirement investments. A 403(b) allows you to invest for retirement with a special boost from the Federal Government.

THE ROLE OF YOUR EMPLOYER. What your employer does in the 403(b) arrangement. Equally important, we will review what the employer does NOT do. Also, what to do if your employer fails to do a good job when it comes to 403(b) plans.

THE ROLES OF THE PRINCIPLE INVESTMENT PROVIDERS, LIFE INSURANCE COMPANIES AND MUTUAL FUNDS. Within 403(b) plans, the investments are invested with either life insurance companies or mutual funds. You will learn how these various types of investments work, and what are the risks and rewards of different types of investments.

HOW TO SHOP AND COMPARE. When choosing investment providers, not all companies are created equal. How to pick and choose in a confusing financial world.

WHERE A 403(b) FITS INTO YOUR FINANCIAL PLANNING. The 403(b) can be the cornerstone of your financial planning, but you need to know how it fits, and what you should do to realize your goals.

HOW TO CALCULATE YOUR MAXIMUM ANNUAL CONTRIBUTIONS. This type of plan gives you more flexibility that other plans when it comes time to make contributions. A step-by-step guide to figuring how much you can defer.

HOW TO MOVE YOUR MONEY AROUND. Another bonus to the 403(b) is your enhanced ability to move your money around. A guide to the rules and reasons behind doing so.

WHAT TO DO WHEN YOU ARE A RETIRED OWNER OF A 403(b). There are millions of retired teachers and nurses who have 403(b) accounts. Here is what to do with them.

This book was written to help the typical user of a 403(b) who usually works for a school, college, charity or hospital. Their 403(b) plan usually gets contributions from the employee, but not from the employer. However, there are two situations where the general rules about 403(b)s may be a little different for some readers. The first is if your employer is a church or church related organization. The second is if your employer is also contributing into your 403(b) plan. The book will mention where the rules differ for those two situations.

Knowledge is power. With a little knowledge, you can make your 403(b) plan a much more powerful tool for your retirement. This book will show you how. At the end of it, I think you will agree that the 403(b) plan is "THE BEST RETIREMENT PLAN AROUND".

CHAPTER TWO

WHAT IS A 403(b) PLAN?

In this chapter we will discuss the basic outline of the 403(b) retirement plan. Points to be discussed include:

*   WHAT IS A 403(b) PLAN?

*   WHAT DO THEY DO?

*   HOW DO YOU GET ONE?

*   WHO IS ELIGIBLE?

*   THE PLAN'S HISTORY

*   THE CURRENT 403(B) MARKET

*   THE FUTURE OF THE 403(b) PLAN

A clear understanding of how the plan works is required if you are to be able to get the maximum benefit out of the plan.

WHAT IS 403(b) PLAN?

A 403(b) is a retirement plan designed to be used by certain types of employees, primarily employees of educational and not-for-profit organizations. This plan is designed to permit the employees to control how much is saved for their retirement. It does so through a method known as tax deferral. The contributions are not taxed at the time the money is earned and placed in the investments. Furthermore, the invested funds will be allowed to grow without being taxed on any current interest or dividends until the funds are withdrawn, usually after the worker has retired. Because of these two tax advantages, money invested in this type of a plan will normally grow much faster than money that would have to be taxed.

The name "403(b)" refers to the section of the Internal Revenue Code which authorizes such plans. Another section of the same code is section 401(k), which authorizes retirement plans for businesses. The 403(b) plan is also sometimes referred to as a "TSA" or a "TDA". A teacher at a school may be told that they can use a "TSA" to save for their retirement. The use of these other names goes back to a time when life insurance companies and others thought that calling something a 403(b) plan was awkward and sounded strange and unappealing. So they called them something else. However, in the last ten years, the increasing popularity of 401(k) plans in the corporate world has made it possible for people to start calling 403(b)s by their technical name.

TSA stands for Tax Saving Annuity or Account, while TDA stands for Tax Deferred Account or Annuity. In reality, these are 403(b) plans. Throughout this book, we will generally refer to these plans by the name 403(b).

The employees who can use the 403(b) plan include teachers, college employees, hospital employees of not-for-profit hospitals, church employees, and employees of certain types of not-for-profit organizations. This type of plan is NOT available to the majority of workers, most of whom work for profit-making businesses. Only these special categories are eligible for 403(b)s.

This plan is of a type known in the retirement plan industry as a "Salary Reduction" plan. Salary Reduction refers to how the plans get their contributions. The money comes from your salary, as opposed to the money coming from an employer's contribution. Other types of salary reduction plans include 401(k)s and SAR/SEP-IRAs. Although all of these varieties share the same basic concept when it comes to funding the plan, they are not identical. Each has a whole range of special rules that set it apart from the others. Many of these differences will be discussed later in this book.

Salary Reduction plans are considered a variation of Defined Contribution plans ("DC"). If you think of a retirement plan as a large pool of water, with DC Plans you know how much is flowing into the pool each month, but not how much will be in the pool when you retire. How much you will receive when you retire will depend not only on how much goes in, but on how much the plan earns over the years, and how much is spent on expenses. Depending on how fast the money grows, and when you leave your employer, you may be better off with a defined contribution plan instead of a pension.

Defined Contribution plans are very different from traditional pensions. Traditional pension plans are called Defined Benefit plans ("DB"). With them, you the employee do not know how much goes into the plan for you, but you know what you will get when you retire (your pension or "benefit"). There is a complicated formula that will tell you how much you will receive each year after you retire, based on your salary and years of service.

In the last ten years or so, Defined Benefit plans (pension plans) have become less popular for employers to offer to their employees. Employers find pension plans very expensive and complicated to operate. The money that goes into a Defined Benefit plan is generally paid out of the employer's pocket, not the employee's. The company can find themselves having to add more and more money to the retirement plan to keep up with the growth in the promised benefits. The company must also employ a team of actuaries to keep track of how much each employee is owed as they move towards retirement.

Defined Benefit plans also have some problems from the employee's standpoint. You may not stay at a employer long enough to receive any benefits from the Plan. You are not usually entitled to any benefit until you have been with an employer a number of years and have become "vested". When you are vested, you are entitled to your benefit even if you than leave the company. However, if an employee change jobs frequently, they may not build up any retirement assets. If you worked for five different employers for four years each, you may end up at the end of twenty years with little or no defined benefit owed to you. Another problem with Defined Benefit Plans compared to Defined Contribution plans is that the employee usually has little or no control over the pension plans. Defined Contribution plans in general, and Salary Reduction plans in particular, give you greater control of the process, including allowing you sometimes to decide on how much money is contributed and how it is invested.

Other types of defined contribution plans include Corporate Profit Sharing Plans, "Money Purchase" Plans, Keogh Plans for small businesses, and SEP-IRAs. All of these plans are used by for-profit businesses. Throughout this book, we will make mention of other types of retirement plans and how they compare to the 403(b). We will make particular comparison to the popular 401(k) plan.

WHAT DO THEY DO?

In a 403(b) plan, your employer will reduce the amount of your paycheck and directly contribute the funds into a special investment account on your behalf. The amount to be withheld is determined by the employees according to their own goals, and according to a special set of IRS rules governing the maximum amount that you can elect to have withheld from your salary. In the eyes of the IRS, you have elected to have your salary reduced, in exchange for the contributions. Thus the name Salary Reduction plan. As a practical matter, most people don't think of it as REduction in their salary, they think of it as a DEduction. In some cases, the employer will also contribute money into your plan, but this is fairly uncommon.

Because the funds are not paid to you, but instead are paid to this special retirement account, you do not have to report them as earnings when computing your income tax. They are not reported by your employer as taxable income when your W-2 is prepared, and your employer does not withhold state or federal income tax on the amounts. When it comes time to fill out your 1040 Form on April 15th, you do not have to show the amount contributed. However, the amount of your contribution is taken into consideration when your FICA (Social Security) contributions are calculated. You will see that your taxable income figure will differ from your social security income figure on your W-2 form.

While the money is held in this special tax-deferred account, it may be invested in a variety of ways. While it remains in the special account, it is not subject to income taxes or capital gains taxes. Taxes paid each year on investments tend to act like a brake on the growth of your investments. Because it is protected by the special plan's tax status, your 403(b) funds can grow more rapidly.

In most cases, the investment choices that you use to invest your funds are provided by outside financial firms, specifically life insurance companies and mutual fund companies. This is in contrast with many pension, profit-sharing, or 401(k) plans, where your employer may actually be in charge of investing the money. However, many of these other retirement plans also make use of outside firms such as life insurance companies, banks, and mutual funds. Under a 403(b), your employer has the responsibility for selecting the outside firms who provide you the investment options.

HOW DO YOU GET ONE?

If you are employed by an eligible employer, you usually contact your payroll, benefits or human resource office for information. They will provide you with information about your investment choices and the salary reduction (or "deferral") process. Depending on your employer, you may be given little more than the name of the investment firm(s) that you may contact for additional information. Other employers may have a great deal of information for you to review, including educational material. You are essentially being asked two questions. The first is how much money do you want withheld? The second is with which life insurance company or mutual fund on the employer's list do you want the money to be invested?

Your employer may provide you with worksheets that can allow you to calculate the maximum amount or percentage you can have withheld under the IRS rules. You may, of course, choose a lesser amount or percentage than the maximum. However, some employers do not provide such a worksheet. In those cases, you will use worksheets provided by the life insurance companies or mutual funds. IRS rules state that you may change your contribution percentage or amount only once a tax year. For most people, the tax year is the same as the calendar year. However, you may stop your contribution at any time. You may also change which life insurance company or mutual fund receives your contributions during the year. The IRS does not set a limit on how often you can make that type of a change.

The choices of investment providers may be as few as one, or as many as a hundred. As will be discussed later in this book, many of these "choices" are very similar, so that for all of the names on the list, you may only have a handful of real alternatives. You must choose by the type of alternative you wish, and the particular provider. For example, you may wish to have the money go into a fixed annuity contract, but you must also select the particular life insurance company. Similarly, you may choose to invest in blue chip stocks through a mutual fund, but you must also pick which specific stock fund to use.

9

Once you have reviewed your materials, you will usually complete several forms. One of these forms will be a form instructing your payroll department to start withholding money from your paycheck and to start depositing it into your new account. This is the "salary reduction" form. Another form will be a form to open up your mutual fund account or life insurance annuity contract. This form will go back to the investment provider.

WHO IS ELIGIBLE?

The IRS has some fairly lengthy rules governing who may take part in a 403(b). However, the basic rules are as follows. If your employer is a public educational organization, or a not-for-profit organization under rule 501(c)1 of the Tax Code, or a church or church related operation, it is most likely able to offer its employees 403(b) plans. So, you are eligible if you work for:

* **A PUBLIC SCHOOL OR SCHOOL DISTRICT**

* **A PRIVATE SCHOOL**

* **A COLLEGE OR UNIVERSITY**

* **A NOT-FOR-PROFIT HOSPITAL**

* **A CHURCH OR RELIGIOUS ORGANIZATION**

* **A CHARITABLE ORGANIZATION**

* **CERTAIN TYPES OF PUBLIC SERVICE ORGANIZATIONS**

All of these types of employers have one thing in common: they are all not-for-profit. If you are employed by a company or organization that is a profit making venture, you are not covered by a 403(b) plan. If you work in the for-profit sector, your employer would normally be eligible for a 401(k) plan.

However, not all not-for-profit employers are eligible. If you work for a Federal, State, or local government employer, you are also not likely to be covered by a 403(b). Federal employees are covered by the Federal Thrift Plan. City and State workers in turn have their own type of deferral retirement plan. That plan is called a 457 Plan. There can be exceptions if your employer is both a local government, and part of the list above. You can have employees of different departments within a city covered by different plans. So city workers who drive street sweepers are not eligible for 403(b)s, although city workers who teach in the schools usually are eligible.

The IRS definition of a public educational employer is as follows:

"A state or local government or any of its agencies or instrumentalities can be a qualified employer. It is a qualified employer only for employees who perform (or have performed) services, directly or indirectly, for an educational organization. For this purpose, an Indian tribal government is a state government. An educational organization is one that normally maintains a regular faculty and curriculum, and normally has a regularly enrolled body of students in attendance at the place where it carries on educational activities."

By IRS definition, administrative, clerical and janitorial workers are considered to perform indirect services for an educational organization, and can be covered by a 403(b).

The IRS description of a not-for-profit, tax exempt organization under Section 501(c)3 is:

"Generally, a qualified employer includes an organization that is tax exempt because it is organized and operated exclusively for religious, charitable, scientific, public safety testing, literary, or educational purposes. It also includes a tax-exempt organization that is organized and operated exclusively to encourage national or international amateur sports competition, or for the prevention of cruelty to children or animals. The organization can be a corporation, community chest, fund, or foundation."

For most readers, the question of whether or not you are an employee is simple. Most readers receive a paycheck and a W-2. However, for a few, there may be a question as to whether or not someone is an employee, or an independent consultant. For example, some doctors at a not-for-profit hospital may fall into a gray area. The IRS has a lengthy set of circumstances to review to determine if someone is an employee or an independent consultant. In particular, a worker who believes that they are an independent contractor or consultant, but who performs ALL of their services for the same organization, should review the IRS criteria.

If your employer ceases to be a qualified employer, you will not be able to continue to contribute to your 403(b). However, your existing 403(b) accounts will remain tax-deferred. You would not need to make any change to them.

11

THE PLAN'S HISTORY

If you read a personal finance magazine, you would think that the whole world revolves around the 401(k) plan. In fact, the 403(b) plan has been around for much longer. The 403(b) was started in 1958. At that time, Congress was concerned that not-for-profit employees were not being given any retirement benefits by their employers. They decided to allow the employees to fund their own retirement plan, even if the employer could not or would not contribute. Thus, the 403(b) was created. It would be many years before a similar arrangement was offered to employees of businesses by the creation of the 401(k) plan.

When the plan was first offered, it was unclear if educational workers were covered. Teachers and other employees of not-for-profit schools were unsure if they were specifically covered by this new type of plan. The law was made clearer in 1961, when the law specifically stated that educational workers were covered.

When the 403(b) was first established, the only acceptable place to deposit your investments was with a life insurance company. Money deposited with life insurance companies for retirement is called an annuity. So most of these plans were known by the name Tax Saving Annuity, TSA. This was a great deal for the life insurance industry, but it left the employees with a small selection of alternatives. In 1974, the law was changed to allow employees to make use of mutual funds as well as life insurance annuities. An account using mutual funds is sometimes called a 403(b)7 account. With this change, the options open to eligible employees were greatly expanded.

Over the last fifteen years, a number of smaller changes have been made to the rules. In fact, every time there is a major revision of the tax code, some changes in the 403(b) rules invariably occur. As a result, the rules for 403(b)s have grown to resemble a patchwork quilt. This is one reason why it is sometimes difficult to figure out the logic behind certain rules. Many of the recent changes were made to bring the 403(b) rules closer to the rules for other types of retirement plans. Hopefully, there will come a time when a simplified set of common rules govern all types of retirement plans.

THE CURRENT 403(b) MARKET

Despite the lack of attention in the media when it comes to 403(b) plans, the current overall market is quite large. Over 250 billion dollars is currently invested in 403(b) plans. The total number of current or retired employees using these plans exceeds four million people. However, many eligible employees do not make use of the plans. Although 403(b) plans provide much of the same benefit as a 401(k) at a corporation, eligible employees at a not-for-profit are only half as likely to use their 403(b) plan compared to 401(k) eligible employees.

Much of the reason for this lower participation arises because there is a lack of basic information for the 403(b) employees to use in making decisions. If 403(b) eligible employees received the same amount of education about their plan as 401(k) employees, it is possible that they would be more likely to contribute.

Because they got an early head start, life insurance companies provide most of the 403(b) plan investments at the present time. It is estimated that over 90% of the money invested in these plans is held by life insurance companies in either fixed or variable 403(b) annuities. Mutual funds have made only a small dent in the marketplace.

THE FUTURE OF THE 403(b) PLAN

Looking into a crystal ball, there are a number of changes that we may see concerning 403(b)s in the next five or ten years. Most of these changes should be for the better.

The first would be the continuing trend to make most of the rules for 403(b)s and other types of retirement plans the same. There is no logical reason why some of the rules are different. The rules evolved in a haphazard manner over the last thirty years. It would reduce confusion if Congress attempted to update and standardize many of the rules.

Another change is that the employers likely will make a more concerted effort to educate their employees about the uses of these plans. As mentioned before, employee use of 403(b)s is only half of that of 401(k)s. Knowing that their employees will need to prepare for their retirements, employers may feel the need to step up their education campaigns. This has already started to happen in the 401(k) market. If employers fail to educate their employees, many of those employees will find themselves with an inadequate retirement. It is possible that the Congress may amend the rules to force not-for-profit employers to take a more active role in this area of education. With adequate information, it is likely that teachers, nurses, and others will make greater use of the 403(b) plan.

A third change will come about as the mutual fund companies move to aggressively battle the life insurance companies for the 403(b) market. Up to now, most mutual fund companies have been content to let the life insurance companies fight it out for this market. The mutual fund industry instead concentrated on individual investors and the 401(k) market. However, they are now making the decision to enter the fray. Because mutual funds are usually a lower cost method of investing compared to life insurance companies, this competition can cause quite a change in the market. If this change leads to lower costs for the employees, then it will be a good development. Some of the names of mutual fund families that you can expect to move into this area include Fidelity, Vanguard, and Scudder.

Although the 403(b) market is currently open to only life insurance companies and mutual funds, there is no logical reason that the law could not be changed to permit other financial services firms, such as banks, savings & loans, credit unions, or stock brokerage firms, to participate as well. All of those financial institutions are currently allowed to handle funds from other types of retirement plans such as 401(k)s. Only 403(b)s remain off limits. There may come a time when you will be able to invest your 403(b) assets in a bank, or with a stockbroker.

One of the most interesting new ideas is the notion that some of the discount stock brokerage firms, such as Charles Schwab & Co., will take an active interest in this market. This could allow a 403(b) investor to purchase a wide range of investments, including no-load mutual funds, in a very low-cost and efficient manner through a discount brokerage firm. For example, you might be able to have a single 403(b) account at a discount brokerage firm, but use the account to invest in a number of mutual funds from different mutual fund families.

Many of these potential changes would benefit the employees greatly. The future of the 403(b) plans looks brighter than ever.

14

CHAPTER THREE

THE BENEFITS OF TAX-DEFERRAL

As with most retirement plans, the major benefit of investing through a 403(b) plan resides in the favorable tax treatment that the plans receive. This tax treatment allows you to accumulate assets for retirement at a faster rate than would normally be the case if you had to pay taxes every year. This chapter will examine this benefit of tax deferral. The key points to be considered are:

* WHAT IS TAX-DEFERRAL?

* HOW USEFUL A TOOL IS IT?

* WHEN DO I PAY MY TAXES?

* HOW CAN I COMPARE TAXABLE VERSUS TAX-DEFERRED INVESTMENTS?

* WHAT IF TAX LAWS CHANGE IN THE FUTURE?

Tax planning is a key part of any financial plan. It is important you understand the tax implications of your 403(b) plan. Much of the discussion in this chapter equally applies to ANY tax-deferred plan such as a 401(k) plan or an IRA.

WHAT IS TAX-DEFERRAL?

The primary advantage of any type of retirement plan is the benefit of TAX-DEFERRAL. Tax-deferral means that you do not pay income taxes on the portion of your salary that you contributed to the plan, nor are you taxed on any of the earnings of the plan while the funds remain invested. You pay taxes when you withdraw the funds, usually many years later during retirement.

This contrasts with taxable investments, where you are taxed as you go. Most investments that you know of are taxable. For example, you must pay taxes on your income before you can take the money and invest it. Once invested, the interest you are paid by your bank or savings & loan, or the interest paid to you by U.S. Government or corporate bonds, is taxable. You also pay taxes on the dividends paid to you by stocks that you own. And when you sell an asset whose price has gone up in value, such as stocks, mutual funds, or real estate, you generally owe capital gains tax on the increase in value in the year of the sale.

You should also not confuse tax-deferred with tax-free. Tax-free would mean that you are never taxed. The only major example of tax-free investing is the interest earned on a municipal bond or municipal bond mutual fund.

The benefit of tax-deferral shows up in two ways. When you earn $100, you would normally have to pay Federal and State income taxes on it. This might leave you with $65. You could then invest that money. Under a tax-deferred plan such as a 403(b), your entire $100 would be invested, not just the $65.

The other facet of tax-deferral occurs year after year as your investment grows. With an ordinary taxable investment, if you invested $100 and earned 9%, or $9, you might lose 1/3 of it to taxes that year. If you were allowing your money to accumulate, you would start the second year with $106. Under tax-deferral, you would not pay taxes on the earnings of the investment each year, so you would start the second year with $109. The interest on your accumulated interest is called compound interest. Over time, the power of compounding is what leads to much of the growth in value of any investment. Because taxes act as a brake on the compounding, a fully taxable investment has more trouble picking up speed.

16

HOW USEFUL A TOOL IS IT?

To understand how useful tax-deferral can be, let us use a simple example. Let us say you have a choice between two options. In the first, you earn $100 and invest it for the next twenty years. Your money will grow at 9% a year.

In the second example, you earn $100, but you are taxed on it. You will also have to pay taxes on the investment's earnings each year. Your combined state and federal tax rate is 35%. You will also invest the money for twenty years.

At the end of twenty years, you will retire. When you retire, you will stop letting the money grow. Instead, you will spend the earnings generated each year to supplement your retirement income.

At the end of twenty years, the first account will have grown to $560. It will earn $50 in the twenty-first year (9% of $560). The second, taxable account will have grown to $202. It will earn $18 in the twenty-first year.

If you withdraw your income out of the retirement account so you may spend it, you will have to pay taxes on it. If you are still in a 35% tax bracket, you will have $32 to spend after subtracting taxes from the $50 from the tax-deferred account. With the taxable account, you will have $11 to spend, after subtracting taxes from the $18. In other words, the tax-deferred investment leaves you with three times as much income when you retire as the taxable version.

Of course, the $560 that you have invested in the first account has never been taxed, while the $202 in the second account has already been taxed. What if you took all of the money in the tax-deferred account out and paid taxes on it? How would it compare? $560 minus 35% taxes would still leave you with $364, after taxes. Remember that the fully taxable account is only $202. You are still much better off than if you had paid taxes each year. The chart below compares taxable versus tax-deferred investing over time.

To use another example, let us consider the example cited at the beginning of Chapter One. This was the 35-year-old teacher whose tax-deferred account grew to over half a million dollars at retirement at age 62. The teacher gave up about $50 a week of take-home pay. If that teacher had instead paid taxes on the money the entire time, their investment would have grown to only $193,000 by age 62.

17

GROWTH OF $10,000 OVER 30 YEARS

	Taxable Account	Tax-Deferred Account	Difference
Year 1:	$10,600	$10,900	$300
Year 10:	$17,908	$23,673	$5,768
Year 20:	$32,071	$56,044	$23,973
Year 30:	$57,434	$132,676	$75,242

Assuming a 9% annual return and combined income tax bracket of 33% (State & Federal).

WHEN DO I PAY MY TAXES?

With almost all tax-deferred investments, you receive the tax protection because your money is invested inside a tax sheltering retirement plan, like a 403(b) or an IRA (Individual Retirement Account). You pay taxes when you remove funds from the retirement plan, usually when you are ready to spend the money. If you have already reached 59 1/2 years of age, then your withdrawal would be considered ordinary income, and taxed like any other income. If you are under 59 1/2, the IRS would tax the withdrawal AND charge you a penalty for withdrawing the money before retirement. However, there are a number of exemptions to that rule (see Chapter 11).

COMPARING TAXABLE VERSUS TAX-DEFERRED

The advantage of tax-deferral seems obvious. As the chart above demonstrated, it can allow your investments to grow twice as fast as ordinary, taxable investments over time. However, there may be certain circumstances where a taxable investment might have an advantage.

One case is when you are not likely to hold an investment for a long period of time. This is particularly important if you are going to use the money before you are 59 1/2, and you may face the extra penalty tax. In those circumstances, you might be better off paying taxes on the investment now, rather than facing the penalties later.

Another example is when there is a special type of investment that you are interested in that is not available or permitted within a tax-deferred retirement plan. For example, many retirement plans do not permit direct investments into real estate, or allow you to invest in commodities or precious metals such as corn futures or gold bullion. If you are interested in making such investments, a tax-deferred retirement plan may be of little help to you.

For most people saving for retirement, a tax-deferred vehicle will work much better than a fully taxable arrangement.

WHAT ABOUT CHANGES IN THE TAX LAW?

One problem faced by investors is attempting to gauge the effect of possible tax law changes in the future. Under some scenarios, deferring taxes into the future could turn out to be worse than paying the taxes now. You might be in a higher tax bracket. However, the opposite could easily be true. That is, you may find your tax situation even better for deferral as a result of changes in the current tax code. You may be in a lower tax bracket. Or you may be able to time it so taxable distributions from your retirement plan are received in years when you have tax deductible losses on other investments or tax deductible expenses. On balance, it is probably unproductive to worry about what changes in the tax code *might* occur. One thing that seems certain is that over time, the tax code will change. But you can only make your decisions based on what you know at the present time.

CHAPTER FOUR

THE ROLE OF YOUR EMPLOYER

The role of the employer in a 403(b) plan is quite different from the role played by an employer in a profit sharing or 401(k) plan. This can be both good and bad, depending on how your employer chooses to fulfill their role. Armed with knowledge about 403(b)s, you can influence how your employer fulfills their role. Key points in this chapter include:

* **WHAT YOUR EMPLOYER DOES IN THE TYPICAL 403(b)**

* **WHO DOES THE RECORD KEEPING?**

* **RELATIONSHIPS WITH INVESTMENT PROVIDERS**

* **THE EMPLOYER'S LEGAL OBLIGATIONS**

* **EXAMPLES OF GOOD AND BAD ARRANGEMENTS**

* **WHAT TO DO IF YOUR EMPLOYER IS A "DUD"**

The greatest obstacle to the 403(b) plan actually fulfilling its role as the "Best Retirement Plan Around" is the failure of many employers to do a responsible job of arranging providers for the plan. However, even the worst arrangements can be quickly improved. This chapter will show you how.

WHAT YOUR EMPLOYER DOES IN THE TYPICAL 403(b)

One of the major differences between 403(b) plans and the 401(k) plans used by many firms is the role of the employer. In order to understand these differences, let us first look at the typical 401(k) at a corporation.

THE 401(k) EMPLOYER

In most cases, a company decides that it wants to offer a retirement plan as a benefit to its employees. Defined Contribution plans, such as 401(k) and profit sharing plans, tend to be cheaper than giving the employees a traditional pension plan (Defined Benefit). The company may further decide to fund the plan primarily with salary reduction contributions from the employees, a 401(k) plan. However, the employer may also contribute its own money to the plan. The employer will go out and set up the retirement plan.

In order to have a plan, a written plan document must be obtained. The company may have a plan custom written, or get one "off the shelf". Then a retirement trust must be set up to receive the contributions and to hold the investments. Investment choices must be decided on by the trustees of the plan. Trustees are often officers of the company, or a bank or trust company hired to act as trustee. The trustees may decide to give the employees some choice in the investments by giving them a list of options and allowing them to pick the choices for their portion of the trust fund, or they may make all the decisions themselves. Retirement assets may be invested with banks, insurance companies, mutual funds, money managers, or into stocks or bonds with a brokerage firm. Finally, someone must do the record keeping.

Companies usually handle these arrangements in one of two ways. The first involves the company hiring a pension administration firm, called a third party administrator, to write the retirement plan document and handle the record keeping. The employer will also hire one or more mutual funds, banks, insurance companies, or brokerage firms to handle the investments. This method is called an "unbundled" plan. The second method involves hiring one firm to do both the record keeping and provide the investments. This is called a "bundled" plan.

A key point here is that the retirement assets belong to the trust fund. The employees are the beneficiaries of the trust and will get their money at some stage, but it is in the control of the trustees. The money is frequently "pooled" into one account, although each employee's share of the pool must be tracked by the record keeper. The employee does not have a direct relationship with the investment providers; the trustees do. Another key point is that under the law, the trustees and the employer have a legal obligation to look out for the interests of the participants. They are considered "fiduciaries". The main law that governs these types of plans is the Employee Retirement Income Security Act of 1974 ("ERISA"). In addition to looking out for the interest of the employees/beneficiaries, a company must also provide both the employees and various government agencies with information about the plan on an ongoing basis. The two U.S. Government agencies who receive reports are the IRS and the Department of Labor.

If a company is smart, it will try to keep the expenses of the plan low. Most or all of the expenses of the plan are paid by the employees one way or another. Keeping expenses low will increase the net return to the employees, and reduce the likelihood of complaints. The company should also avoid investment providers that charge the plan sales charges, or "loads", on the money invested. Because the investment providers are able to handle the employees on a group basis, often any sales charges are waived. From the standpoint of the investment provider, they only had to make one sale to get the business, even if there are 500 employees. Only a careless employer will stick his or her employees with unnecessary expenses and sales charges, although it does happen. In particular, small, less sophisticated employers often get sold an expensive set of investment options by a stockbroker or insurance agent.

How does the 403(b) employer differ from the 401(k) employer? Let us look at the typical 403(b) plan.

THE 403(b) EMPLOYER

The employees work for an IRS qualified organization, such as a school district, and are eligible to use 403(b) plans. The employer than arranges for one or more life insurance companies or mutual funds to offer 403(b) accounts to their employees. It is acceptable under the law for an employer to permit any number of potential investment providers. Employees may choose to participate in the plans, or they may decline. However, the employer does not have much connection with, or responsibility for, the investment providers. An employer can contribute to its employee's 403(b) accounts, but it is rare that they actually do so. Most employers that contribute money towards their employee's retirement do so by putting the money into another type of defined contribution plan or into a defined benefit plan (pension) instead of a 403(b).

22

The accounts that are set up typically belong to the individual employee. Each life insurance company or mutual fund keeps track of the investments made by the employees with them. If an employee decides to take advantage of this plan, the employer's payroll department will withhold the designated amount from the employee's salary and send it to the life insurance company or mutual fund. If the employee decides to stop contributing, the payroll department stops the withholding. But once the money leaves the employer and is sent to the investment provider, the employer usually has no more dealings with it. Each employee's account belongs solely to the employee, not to the school district or to a retirement trust fund.

Essentially, a 403(b) employer only does two things regarding the plans. First, they decide which life insurance companies or mutual funds can offer accounts to their employees. Second, their payroll department handles the withholding. Beyond that, employers have little else to do with the plans. The only costs incurred by most 403(b) employers is the cost of having payroll handle the withholding and forwarding of the funds. In these days of computers and automation, this is a minor item. An employer may also spend money on educating the employees about retirement issues and promoting the retirement plan. Employers do not want to be seen as pushing one investment over another, but they may try to give the employees an idea of what their options are all about so that the employees may be able to make a more informed decision. However, many employers have chosen to spend nothing on educating their employees.

So there are two major differences between the 401(k) setup and the 403(b) setup. First, the 403(b) employer is NOT setting up the retirement plan and a trust fund. Instead, each employee has their own individual arrangement with the life insurance company or mutual fund. The employer is merely making the arrangement available. Secondly, the 403(b) employer is not obligated under the law to look after the best interest of their employees. Surprisingly enough, 403(b) plans do not generally fall under the ERISA law. The employers are not considered a fiduciary in regards to this type of retirement plan, and are generally not held accountable for doing a poor job. Furthermore, they do not have to provide reports to the employees or to the U.S. Government.

A major exception to the ERISA coverage is a case in which the employer also contributes to the employee's 403(b) plan, or otherwise exercises an unusual amount of control with the 403(b) accounts. In those cases, the 403(b) will fall under the jurisdiction of ERISA. However, most employers do not contribute to their employee's 403(b)s and avoid having much control over the plans. Remember, even if your employer does contribute money towards your retirement, it only counts towards making the 403(b) plans subject to ERISA if they are putting the money into your 403(b). For example, if a not-for-profit hospital contributes money into a separate plan, such as a pension plan, it doesn't make the 403(b) subject to ERISA. Most employers want to avoid being subject to ERISA so that they can reduce their level of responsibility and record-keeping.

However, despite usually being able to avoid responsibility for a 403(b) plan, the employer still gets to decide which life insurance companies or mutual funds can offer 403(b) accounts to their employees. In other words, who is on the "approved list". The law states that limiting the choices to a small number of investment providers that the employees may select from does not make the employer or the plan subject to ERISA. This creates a major problem. Some employers do an excellent job of screening for investment providers, but, unfortunately, many do a terrible job.

EMPLOYERS AND INVESTMENT PROVIDERS

There are three common employer approaches used in the 403(b) world. Here are examples of these approaches.

In the first arrangement, the administrators of a school district with 500 teachers decide that they do not want to be held accountable for doing a bad job with the 403(b)s. Furthermore, they wish to avoid any possibility of being seen exercising control over the plan. So they decide that any life insurance company or mutual fund that approaches them can be on the approved list. This way, nobody will blame them for anything that happens.

The result is that a teacher may find a bewildering array of fifty life insurance companies and ten mutual fund families being offered to them at their school district. The life insurance companies may offer both fixed accounts and variable (mutual fund) accounts. Each mutual fund family may also offer five to fifty different funds. It would seem that the teacher has choices galore!

Why is that a problem? Because this method is so chaotic and inefficient, the only life insurance companies and mutual funds who will usually bother to get on the list are ones who charge a lot of money in expenses and sales charges. Low cost investment firms tend to shy away from this market because there is no way to contact employees in a cost efficient manner. Even if a school district has 500 employees, a low cost investment provider must still find a way to contact the teachers one by one and explain the benefits of their choice. At the same time, sixty other firms are also yelling out their message. Because of this, many no-load mutual fund families do not bother trying to get on a school district list (no-load mutual funds are funds sold without sales charges, called "loads"). The list ends up being almost entirely load mutual funds and load life insurance companies.

Most teachers end up buying their 403(b) from one of a legion of life insurance agents who sell the annuities, one by one, to the teachers in the school break room. Those life insurance agents receive large sales commissions for selling the accounts, but those commissions come from the pockets of the teachers. Because of those high commissions, it is worthwhile for the agents to track the teachers down one by one. An employee seems to have endless choices, but all of the choices turn out to be high priced.

The second arrangement involves an employer, perhaps a hospital or college, who decides to limit the selection to one or two life insurance companies, and one or two mutual fund families. This arrangement looks somewhat like the 401(k) arrangement. Because the investment providers are being given an exclusive, or near exclusive, opportunity to provide investments on a group basis, any sales charges are frequently waived. So under the second method, employees pick their mutual funds or annuities, but usually avoid paying the sale charges that those in the first arrangement generally get stuck with when investing. Even with only a few investment providers to select from, the employees still have dozens of choices. Furthermore, the employer is still not deemed to be in "control", and thus subject to ERISA, by limiting the investment providers to one or two companies.

The third arrangement is usually found with very large organizations, such as a state-wide public school teacher retirement system or a major college. In this arrangement, the plan is set up to look almost exactly like a large 401(k) plan. The employer might hire an independent record keeper who may also be the master custodian of the plan. The employer may also select a number of different mutual funds and life insurance companies to provide the investment options. In these cases, the employee does not have any separate dealings with the various mutual funds and life insurance companies. All of their dealings are with the single record keeper. Because of the size and negotiating strength of the sponsoring organization, they can usually arrange a very low cost deal for their employee participants. They also usually analyze the investment choices carefully before putting them on the list. Surprisingly enough, even this type of plan may not be subject to ERISA.

It would appear that in the first example, the teachers would be better off because of the greater range of choice. However, the range of choices is misleading. Just because there are fifty life insurance companies doesn't mean you really have fifty different choices. Most of the choices being offered are very much like the others. In reality, there may only be a handful of real alternatives. It is a bit like the offers you get for credit cards in the mail. You may get mail from 50 different banks during the year offering you a credit card. But when you sit down and analyze the offers, you realize that all of the them look fairly similar. In fact, there is only a small number of factors that vary from card to card (interest rate, annual fee, grace period, credit limit). So the fifty offers end up representing only four or five variations.

The result is that an employee in a 403(b) plan under one of the other two arrangements can still have enough options to put together a diversified, balanced portfolio, even though it appears at first glance that they don't have nearly as many choices. However, because of the inefficient nature of the first arrangement, it tends to be much more expensive for the employee than the other two methods. From the standpoint of the employer, the liability and responsibility is pretty much the same under all three methods. Furthermore, the cost of withholding the salary reduction and forwarding it to the investment companies is pretty much the same.

WHAT IF YOU HAVE A "DUD"?

Given a choice, most employees would be better off if they were given the option of investing in a smaller selection of low cost investments offered without sales charges. In other words, you would prefer the second or third arrangement mentioned above. One or two "no-load" mutual fund families, and one or two low cost life insurance companies, are all you really need to have enough options to create a good investment portfolio. If your employer gives you such an arrangement, congratulations.

What should you do if your employer gives you nothing but high expense, sales charge "loaded" investments? What should you do if are offered the first arrangement mentioned above? Or you are offered the second arrangement, but you are still faced with sales charges or high expenses?

The first thing you need to understand is that there is no valid reason why you should have to put up with a poor selection of investment options. If you approach your employer's human resource or benefits office, they will often give you various reasons why they can't or won't change. Usually they say it is because it will cost the employer money, or that it will create legal problems.

However, it will not cost your employer any more money to give you a good selection as to give you a bad selection. The cost of the withholding by the payroll department has nothing to do with who gets the money. Furthermore, the employer is generally not subject to ERISA and the reporting requirements.

Also, there is usually no legal reason why you should be stuck with these choices. Managers will make vague sounds about "employer liability", or how they are bound to the current arrangement by contract. In reality, the risk to the employer is greater when they do a poor job, not when they do a better job. The claims of potential liability ring hollow. And as a general rule, the employer has no contractual arrangement with the investment firms. If the employer wants to allow new options on the list, the current investment providers are powerless to interfere. In fact, quite often the administrators made an uninformed selection, and simply do not want to admit it to the employees.

The first thing you should do is examine your current arrangement. Pay particular attention to costs and sales charges. As you will find out in later chapters, a fancy name or a hot performance record does not excuse high expenses and sales charges.

If you are being hit with high fees and charges, you should contact your human resource or benefits office and find out if there is a procedure to add choices. If there is, find out what it is and follow it. In order to add a choice, you may need more than one interested employee to comply with the procedure. With luck, you can get at least one family of low-cost, no-load choices on the list. After you have finished reading this book, you should be able to find an acceptable addition to the approved list. Most mutual funds or life insurance companies will be happy to be placed on the approved list if some employees ask for them.

If your employer has opted for the second arrangement, a very short list of investment providers, you may not even have to add a new investment firm or drop the old firm to get rid of the sales charges. Here's why. Most mutual fund families, even those that sell their funds through stockbrokers and insurance agents and levy sales charges on investments, will waive those fees for a large retirement plan. That is the arrangement your employer SHOULD have made when they put the mutual fund family on the approved list. Instead, they were probably talked into using the funds, with sales charges, by a local insurance agent or stockbroker (who just happens to be the person who is paid those sales charges).

To rectify this situation, the employer can contact the mutual fund family directly and inform them that if sales charges are not waived in the future, the employer will remove them from the approved list. If a mutual fund family is on a short list of investment providers for a large employer they will, after much hemming and hawing, usually drop the sales charges. This will, of course, make the local insurance agent or stockbroker unhappy, as they will lose out on future sales commissions. By the same token, it will make the employees that much better off.

If your employer uses the first arrangement, and there is not a procedure to add investment choices, you will have to pressure your employer to create one. Remember, there is no valid legal or financial reason for them to deny you. You may need to get another employee involved. If the employer makes the argument that they don't want too many choices on the approved list, then tell them to dump one of the high cost choices to make room! Any employer who has fifty life insurance companies or mutual funds with sales charges on their approved list could easily dump half of them, add one choice without sales charges, and have a better list than they had before.

Most people don't like being seen as a troublemaker. However, it is your money that is being spent on sales charges, not the employer's. If you and the rest of the employees are losing 5% of your contributions to some life insurance agents or stock brokers, it can add up to a lot of money. For example, a school district with 500 employees might have 200 employees who contribute an average of $4,000 a year into their 403(b)s. That means a total of $800,000 a year goes towards their 403(b)s. If 5% of that is paid out in the form of sales commissions, that means $40,000 a year is redirected into the pockets of the life insurance agents and stockbrokers. That money is lost forever by the employees. As you will learn in the following chapters, many investment sellers who claim to not charge a sales commission simply hide it in the calculations. Remind all of the other employees of that and you may find someone else willing to be the rabble-rouser.

If you are unable to change your employer's mind, you have only two choices. The first is to not participate in a 403(b) at all. Even despite high costs, the benefits of a 403(b) are such that not using it at all is probably not a great option. The second choice is to select the best of a bad lot. You may just have to grit your teeth and live with it for a while. However, as you will learn later in the book, you do not have to LEAVE your money with the chosen investment provider.

CHAPTER FIVE

THE INVESTMENT PROVIDERS

One of the major differences between 403(b) plans and other types of retirement plans is the limitation on who can be given the investment assets. In this chapter, we will review that issue, and show that it does not significantly impact your options. Areas to be covered include:

     *   **INVESTMENT RULES FOR 403(b) PLANS**

     *   **THE ROLE OF THE INVESTMENT PROVIDER**

     *   **THE ROLE OF THE CUSTODIAN**

     *   **HOW OTHER RETIREMENT PLANS OPERATE**

     *   **WHY THE "LIMITATION" IS A NON-ISSUE**

     *   **INVESTMENT PROVIDER: FRIEND OR FOE**

The key to the success of any retirement plan is the ability of the invested funds to grow over time. This is why the investment providers are the key to the whole process. It is crucial that you understand what they do, and how they do it. Furthermore, you must know whether they are your friend or your enemy.

INVESTMENT RULES FOR 403(b) PLANS

The funds deferred in a 403(b) arrangement may only be invested in two types of investment vehicles. This is different from other types of retirement plans, which may make use of a wider range of investment options.

The first option is to invest the funds with a life insurance company in a "fixed" or "variable" annuity contract. A fixed annuity is one in which the life insurance company accepts the funds as a deposit, and pays a fixed interest rate on them. That interest rate may change over time, but the value of your invested principal remains the same. A variable annuity is a life insurance company's version of a mutual fund. Either version of these investments is known under the tax code as a 403(b)1 arrangement.

The second place that the funds may be invested is with mutual funds. A 403(b) account with a mutual fund must be set up with a "custodian", just like an IRA (Individual Retirement Account). This version is known under the tax code as a 403(b)7 arrangement.

There are two exceptions to the rules mentioned above. The first is for employees of churches or church related organizations. In addition to the options of using mutual funds or annuities, employees of these church groups may also use a "retirement income account" to invest in a wider range of investments. This arrangement looks very much like a 401(k) defined contribution plan.

The second exception is some employers have alternate arrangements in which they operate investment pools that function like a mutual fund or a fixed annuity, but are not actually registered mutual funds or annuities. These plans were usually started a number of years ago when the rules where different and are permitted by the IRS under a "grandfathered" exception. That means that the IRS will permit these old exceptions to keep operating, but they will not allow new exceptions. This arrangement is fairly rare, although some large employers have such exceptions.

THE ROLE OF THE INVESTMENT PROVIDER

In most 403(b) arrangements, the investment provider is performing three functions. The first is to provide the actual investment(s) to be used by the plan. They hold the assets of the plan and invest it. The life insurance company takes the deposit and pays interest on the money if the annuity is a fixed one. The mutual funds and life insurance company variable annuities invest the money into stocks and bonds.

The second function that the investment firm provides is the responsibility for the record keeping. As you may recall, your employer generally has no responsibility for the money once they have forwarded it to your investment provider. Once it is there, the investment provider must keep track of what you have invested and earned while you have the account.

The third function is that they are responsible for overseeing distributions of funds from the plan to you, or to another 403(b) account, or to an IRA (Individual Retirement Account). Because this is a tax-deferred plan, the IRS receives reports when funds are taken from the plan, just as they do when you withdraw funds from an IRA. This way they can make sure that investors are claiming the withdrawals as taxable income when appropriate. It is the responsibility of the investment provider to file the appropriate reports with the IRS.

As part of record keeping, the investment providers will provide you with periodic reports showing how your account is doing. These reports may be sent annually, quarterly, or monthly. It will vary with the company. You usually get more frequent reports from the mutual fund companies compared to life insurance companies. When you take a distribution from the plan, they will send you, and the IRS, a "1099-R" form showing exactly how much you received. You use such a report to prepare your taxes.

As a general rule, when you use a life insurance company as your investment provider, the life insurance company will hold the assets and handle the record keeping themselves. With a mutual fund, there will be a custodian to handle some of these functions.

THE ROLE OF THE MUTUAL FUND CUSTODIAN

The role of a retirement plan custodian in a 403(b)7 arrangement is the same as the role of a custodian in an IRA (Individual Retirement Account). When you invest money in an IRA, the account is actually registered in the name of a custodian, who holds the assets for your benefit. The custodian is usually a bank or trust company. The reason the account is not in your name is because the IRA is tax-deferred funds. You may not have ready access to the tax-deferred money without being liable for the taxes. If the mutual fund account was in your name, the IRS would consider the funds to already be in your possession (this is a tax concept known as "constructive receipt", meaning that for all intents and purposes, you already have the money). By having a custodian hold the funds for your benefit, the issue of constructive receipt is avoided. As an example, you may see your IRA account actually titled "ABC Bank as custodian for John Q. Smith, IRA".

The same arrangement is used with 403(b)7 plans. A custodian holds the account for your benefit. They are also responsible for the reporting to the IRS of distributions. As a practical matter, you may never have any real dealings with the mutual fund's custodian. Most funds handle all the paperwork and your dealings with the custodian may be limited to seeing their name on the statements and being charged a small annual custodial fee. Your account might be registered as "ABC Bank as custodian for Mary R. Smith, 403(b)7 Account".

An obvious question is why don't you have a custodian when you place your funds with a life insurance company? The answer is that you have a contract with the life insurance company, but you don't really have any assets. Unlike a mutual fund, where the assets of the fund belong to the shareholders, the assets purchased with an annuity belong to the life insurance company (see Chapter 6 and 7). The issue of constructive receipt only comes up when the life insurance company sends you a check for a distribution.

HOW OTHER RETIREMENT PLANS OPERATE

One difference between 403(b) plans and other types of retirement plans is that 403(b)s may only chose between life insurance companies and mutual funds. You may not, for example, invest 403(b) funds with a bank or stockbroker, except to purchase annuities and mutual funds.

Other types of plans, such as pension plans, profit sharing plans, and 401(k)s, can use a wider range of choices. For example, they can invest money with banks and savings & loans, buy individual stocks and bonds, purchase real estate, or turn the money over to a money manager to invest.

You will remember that with other types of retirement plans, the funds are usually held in a trust fund. The trustees are responsible for the investing of the funds, and the assets purchased are usually registered in the name of the trust. In a sense, the trustees are acting as the custodian of the assets, preventing you from receiving constructive receipt and being liable for taxes until some point in the future when the trustees send you a check for a distribution. The trustees must also report distributions to the IRS (Form 1099-R). Also, unlike most 403(b) arrangements, the trustees are bound by ERISA rules and have a great deal of additional reporting to perform.

IS THE "LIMITATION" ON INVESTMENTS BY A 403(b)s AN ISSUE?

An investor might wonder if the limitations imposed on 403(b) investments, compared to the limitations on other types of retirement plans, are a handicap. The quick answer is no. In reality, the choices available from life insurance companies and mutual funds cover almost the entire investment spectrum.

For example, there are over 6,000 different mutual funds. You can break those funds down into over twenty or more categories. If anything, the choices are so great that it can be difficult to make an informed decision. It would be hard to make a case that investors are at any real disadvantage compared to participants in other types of retirement plans.

In fact, many of the choices you are not permitted to use in a 403(b) plan are some of the investment categories that have been major problems for individual investors in the past. It is very difficult to suffer very large losses (defined as losses of 50% to 100%) in a retirement account using only mutual funds and fixed and variable annuities. However, many investors who invested in individual stocks, low rated "junk" bonds, real estate limited partnerships, precious metals, options or commodities (often at the suggestion of some "expert" at a brokerage firm), have seen huge losses in these other types of investments. This is not to say that it is impossible to lose money in mutual funds and annuities. You most definitely can! It is just very unlikely that you would see a huge loss. You will find that many of the types of investments that are not open to 403(b) investors are those that contain the greatest amount of risk.

Furthermore, most professional money managers believe that all you really need to have in the way of a reasonable selection is as few as four or five different alternatives. That does not mean four or five different families of mutual funds, each with a range of 20 or 30 choices. They are referring to four or five individual mutual funds or annuities, as long as they are of different types. So if you can pick from a selection that includes a fixed annuity, a money market fund, one or two bond mutual funds of different types, and two or three stock mutual funds with different styles, you may have enough choices to do an excellent job of creating an investment portfolio.

INVESTMENT PROVIDERS: FRIEND OR FOE?

Investment firms in general, and life insurance companies in particular, spend a lot of money on advertising. A good deal of the message that they try to get across is that they are your "friend", and you should just trust them. If you give them your money, they will take care of you.

Unfortunately, none of the above is true. Investment firms are in the business of making money. They make their money, like any other business, off their customers. That's you! Although they like their customers to have a warm feeling about the company, the truth is that they are firm that you are buying a product or service from, not your best friend. Much of that advertising is an attempt to build name recognition. With good name recognition, it is easier to sell you something because you are diverted from the important issue of "is it a good deal for me", to an irrelevant issue of how well known is the company you are considering. You should view your choice of investment provider in much the same way as you view your choice of long distance telephone company, by comparing costs and service.

As you will see in the next two chapters, the exact relationship that you have depends on the type of investment provider you chose. Never forget that it's your money you are dealing with, not the life insurance company's or mutual fund's. You should approach all dealings with investment firms with the thought that you are looking out for yourself.

CHAPTER SIX

ANNUITIES

Currently, the majority of the $250 billion dollars in 403(b) assets is held by life insurance companies. If you have a 403(b) account right now, the odds favor that it is with a life insurance company. It is vital that you understand what you have, and what it costs you. Only then can you determine if it is what you need or want. The key areas to know are:

* **WHAT IS A LIFE INSURANCE COMPANY?**

* **HOW DO THEY OPERATE?**

* **WHAT IS A FIXED ANNUITY?**

* **WHAT IS A VARIABLE ANNUITY?**

* **WHAT ARE THE RISKS INVOLVED?**

* **WHO DOES THE INSURANCE AGENT WORK FOR?**

* **HOW MUCH DOES IT ALL COST?**

* **EVALUATING AND SELECTING ANNUITIES**

As you will learn, there is nothing inherently wrong with dealing with a life insurance company with your 403(b). HOWEVER, you must be aware of the potential disadvantages and risks involved when investing with life insurance companies.

WHAT IS A LIFE INSURANCE COMPANY?

Although life insurance companies are a standard feature of the financial landscape, it is amazing how many people do not really understand how they work. It is important that you understand what they are and are not. Let's start with the basics.

Insurance companies come in two major varieties. The first type is Property and Casualty companies. These insurance companies protect you against damage to your property, automobile, business, etc. They act like the reverse of a race track bookie. The property insurance company collects premiums (bets) based on the odds of a loss occurring. But unlike a bookie, who pays the winners, the insurance company pays the losers.

The other major type of insurance company is a Life Insurance company. They are engaged in two main lines of business. The first is life insurance itself. This is similar to property & casualty insurance. They collect premiums from a large number of people, and only pay out on those who die. It is true that, sooner or later, all of their policy holders will die. But the life insurance company sets their rates high enough so that they still make money after they pay off the beneficiaries.

The other line of business that life insurance companies are involved in is providing for people's retirement. They do this by selling an investment vehicle known as an "annuity".

The true meaning of an annuity is a stream of payments made to someone over a period of time. For example, when you retire, your pension from a Defined Benefit plan would be considered an annuity. An annuity arrangement that is currently paying out cash to the policyholder or owner is called an "immediate" annuity. However, there is another version of an annuity where instead of paying out funds, the annuity grows in value. This is called a "deferred" annuity. Deferred annuities can, at a later date, be converted into immediate annuities ("annuitized").

Annuities are sometimes sold to people one at a time and the individual has a copy of the policy. These are called an individual annuity. Annuities are also sold to groups of people, such as all the employees of a hospital or college. There may be a master policy in the name of the employer. This arrangement is called a group annuity. For most people who have 403(b) annuities, you have either an individual or a group deferred annuity. In other words, you are not currently receiving a set payment for the rest of your life from the life insurance company. Instead, your annuity is growing in value until you use the money in the future. Unless otherwise stated, we will be referring to deferred annuities in this book. Deferred annuities are designed to be tax-deferred retirement vehicles.

HOW DO LIFE INSURANCE COMPANIES OPERATE?

Life insurance companies make money the same way as any other business. They sell a service or product at a higher price than it costs them to provide it. When they do the calculations for how much you will receive from any given policy, they always build in an amount of overhead and profit for themselves.

It may be helpful if you understand that there are three major divisions of a life insurance company. One division has to design the life insurance policy or annuity that the company will sell. They need to pay particular attention to the cost of the various policies. They have to take into consideration factors such as mortality (death) rates, marketing and sales efforts, how much interest they pay out, and how much the company can make on the invested premiums (payments).

The second division of the company takes the money paid to the company in premiums and invests it until it is needed to pay benefits under a life insurance policy or an annuity policy. The life insurance company needs to earn more on the invested premiums than the first group's formulas indicate that the policies cost them (this difference is called the "spread"). Life insurance companies invest the money in a wide range of investments, including stocks, real estate and mortgages. However, they use bonds of various sorts as their primary investment option. That is because bonds generally pay a steady, predictable amount of interest from when they are bought until they mature.

This allows the life insurance company to "match" the interest and average length of time until maturity of their bonds with the interest and average length of time on the various policies they have sold. For example, if they calculate that the money given to them for various life insurance policies and annuities will stay with them, on average, for about ten years (until the policy owner dies or cashes out the policy), they will most likely own bonds with an average maturity of ten years. If the bonds pay them an average of 8% a year, and the policies are paid an average of 6% a year, they have a good match and a 2% spread.

Finally, the company must have a sales and marketing division to go out and sell the policies. Few industries are as driven by sales as the life insurance industry. It does not matter how great a policy you have developed, you have to get people to buy it. For a variety of reasons, people have a tendency to avoid thinking about unpleasant concepts such as death. Most people are unlikely to want to run out and by life insurance on their own as life insurance should properly be called "death" insurance. So life insurance companies usually rely on both advertising and a network of commission-based salespeople to push their products. Life insurance companies usually become large and successful based on their ability to sell their policies, not on how well they handle the other components of the business.

Assuming that they have sold a large number of life or annuity policies, the life insurance company makes money on them in various ways. In the case of life insurance itself, they charge more than the actual risk involved and keep the difference. For example, if based on mortality charts the odds of a 35 year old dying this year is one in one hundred, the actual mortality "cost" to an insurer of providing $100 worth of life insurance to a 35 year old is $1 (they would have to charge $1 to one hundred insured 35 year olds to pay off the one who actually dies). So if they charge $1.50 per $100 of coverage, they collect $150 and have enough to cover their overhead and a profit. As long as they insure a large enough sample of people, and avoid insuring only deep-sea divers or race car drivers, they will be able to predict quite accurately how many of their policyholders will die each year. Although the math behind these calculations is very complicated, the basic process is simple. They also make money on the use of the premiums between the time they are received by the life insurance company and the time benefits are paid out.

But how does a life insurance company make money on providing retirement plans to people? That depends on whether or not the deferred annuity is a "fixed" annuity or a "variable" annuity.

WHAT IS A FIXED ANNUITY?

A fixed annuity is a tax-deferred retirement deposit made to a life insurance company. It is not all that different than depositing money in the bank in a Certificate of Deposit (C.D.). Let us first look at what really happens when you deposit money at the bank.

Let's say you walk into the bank and give them $10,000 for a 1-year certificate of deposit. The bank takes your money and gives you a promise to pay you back $10,000 plus a certain amount of interest at the end of one year, say 6%. The bank than takes the $10,000 and invests it by making a loan or buying an investment. They need to earn more than 6% to make a profit. In fact, because of their overhead, they will need to earn

2%-3% more than they pay out (the "spread"). If they are successful in this, they make money. If they are unsuccessful, they still owe you your investment plus interest.

An important point to remember is that what you own is their promise to pay. The actual asset bought by the bank belongs to the bank (which means it ultimately belongs to the bank's shareholders). If all goes well, at the end of the year the bank gives you your $10,000 plus interest. Of course, they may make you a new offer for another year at a new interest rate. Interest paid by banks is normally fully taxable.

Banks traditionally borrow money from depositors for fairly short periods of time, typically one year or less. They also tend to invest their money in fairly short term investments. If you borrow money short-term and lend it short-term, you have a "match". This is like the life insurance company example with the 10-year bonds. A mismatch occurs when you borrow and invest money over different time horizons. This can be risky. An example of a mismatch would occur if a bank borrowed money short-term, selling 1-year C.D.s paying 6%, and used the money to invest long-term, buying 20-year bonds paying 8%. As long as short-term rates stay low, the bank is not in trouble. But if short-term rates rise a great deal next year, the bank could find itself having to pay 8%-9% or more to keep 1-year deposits from moving at renewal. But the bank is still only making 8% on the 20-year bonds. The bank is in trouble (an industry-wide mismatch between short-term deposits and long-term mortgages is what actually started the decline of the savings & loan industry).

A life insurance company selling fixed annuities is doing much the same as the bank. You deposit $10,000 with the life insurance company and they promise to pay you a certain amount of interest. They then invest the money in something, usually bonds, that pay them more than what they pay you. If they are successful, they make money. If they are unsuccessful, they still owe you your investment plus interest.

Once again, the assets that the life insurance company bought belong to the company. You own the promise to pay. Unlike banks, which deal with a lot of short-term depositors, life insurance companies selling annuities are only dealing with people who are investing for retirement or other long-term goals. Under the Tax Code, the interest on these annuities is tax-deferred. As a result, the annuity can be designed for a longer period of time than 1 year. With a typical fixed annuity, the life insurance company usually offers you a multi-year arrangement. They can offer you a higher rate than the bank because they can make longer-term, and hopefully more profitable, investments.

40

For example, a fixed annuity might pay you 7% a year for 5 years, tax-deferred. If the bank is only paying 6% for 1 year, and it's taxable, an investor saving for retirement might choose the insurance annuity. This way they can lock in a higher rate, and get the advantage of tax-deferral. As long as they don't need the money in the next 5 years, this may be a better investment. Someone saving to buy a car next year would, of course, choose the bank.

Some fixed annuities work like the example above. However, most fixed annuities actually offer you a multi-year, variable rate arrangement. For example, you still deposit money with them for 5 years, but the initial interest rate they offer is only guaranteed for the first year. For years 2 through 5, you may receive a higher or lower rate. The life insurance company will have a minimum rate that they can't go below, say 4%, but how much you get above that depends on the life insurance company. So you will receive 7% for the first year, but you might get 6% or 8% in the following year. It depends on what happens to interest rates, and how the life insurance company decides to handle renewal rates.

This creates a potential problem. An unscrupulous life insurance company might try to entice you with a high first year rate, and than drop the rate in the following years. Remember that after the first year, your minimum guaranteed rate might be only 4%. The first year "teaser" rate will allow them to attract a large amount of deposits from unwary investors. After they have locked you in for five or seven years, the company can pay you a below average rate and make back the high first year costs. Thus if the average rate for similar annuities at a given time is 7%, you should be careful if any life insurance company is offering 8% or more.

Most life insurance companies try to be more consistent with their rates. They do this because if they treat their policy holders well, the policyholders will not take their money to the competition. One safeguard that you will find in many policies is a "bail-out" rate. You may be offered an initial rate of 8%, and a minimum rate of 4%. If the rate in any given year drops below 7%, you would be given the option of taking out your money, without penalty, or accepting the new rate. This is the bailout option. If interest rates in general have declined, you may accept the new, lower rate because it is in line with your other choices. However, if the company is no longer offering a competitive rate, you may have an opportunity to move. As a rule, an annuity with a bail-out option is a better choice than a similar annuity without one.

WHAT IS A VARIABLE ANNUITY?

A variable annuity is an annuity that invests in mutual funds. A life insurance company usually sets up its own family of special, variable annuity mutual funds. These funds are very similar to ordinary mutual funds but there are a few differences. For example, the mutual funds in the variable annuity may only be purchased through the annuity.

The variable annuity may offer anywhere from five to twenty different mutual funds as investment options. You might have a money market fund, several bond funds, and a number of stock funds as part of your annuity. There may even be a fixed annuity option tied in with the variable annuity.

When you buy an ordinary mutual fund, you pay for the operating costs of the fund. You may also pay a sales charge, which usually goes to the stockbroker who sold you the mutual fund. With a variable annuity, you pay one set of expenses for the operation of the variable annuity mutual fund. You also pay a second set of expenses to the life insurance company for the plan being an annuity. And you may still pay a sales charge. Generally speaking, a variable annuity 403(b) investment will be more expensive than a similar mutual fund 403(b) investment.

In a fairly recent development in the annuity market, a life insurance company might team up with an outside mutual fund group. In these instances, the life insurance company provides the annuity contract portion of the arrangement with its tax-deferral advantage, while the mutual fund family actually runs the variable annuity mutual funds.

Because variable annuities are a mixture of a life insurance annuity and a mutual fund, they are regulated by the Insurance Commissioners of the various States and by a Federal agency, the S.E.C. (Securities and Exchange Commission). By comparison, fixed annuities and life insurance policies are not regulated by the Federal government. In fact, generally speaking, insurance companies are not subject to Federal regulations. They are governed by the regulations of the various states in which they do business.

Because of the similarity between mutual funds and variable annuities, we will discuss both types of investments in the next chapter.

WHAT ARE THE RISKS INVOLVED IN ANNUITIES?

The risk of an annuity depends on which of the two types of annuities you purchase.

There are three major risks involved when you purchase a fixed annuity. The first is the risk that the life insurance company will not be able to fulfill their promise to pay you your principal and interest as stated. This is the "default" risk. Remember that the life insurance company took your deposit and invested the money. If they lose money on the investments, they may not be able to make good on the promises.

For example, say ABC Life Insurance Company has $5,000,000 of capital. This money belongs to its shareholders. The money came from when the company started and stock was sold to the shareholders, and from retained profits from prior years. ABC takes in $95,000,000 from annuity policy holders. It may be paying them an average interest rate of 6% per year on their deposits. The company will need to earn more than 6% to cover their overhead and make a profit. A prudent life insurance company might invest the $100,000,000 total in bonds with high credit ratings, paying an average of 8%. The company will also match the length of time of the bonds to the expected length of time that the annuities will be on deposit. It is unlikely that such a conservative approach will get them in trouble. Furthermore, the $5,000,000 of shareholder equity provides a safety cushion for the depositors.

But let's say they decided to invest in riskier, low rated bonds ("junk" bonds). These bonds pay the life insurance company 10%. If all goes well, the life insurance company will make even more money. But let's say that a large number of those bonds don't pay off. Although the life insurance company owes policy holders $95,000,000, plus 6% interest, their investments may only be worth $90,000,000. The shareholders equity is wiped out and the life insurance company is insolvent.

At this stage, the insurance regulators for the state where the company is based will have seized control of the company. They probably will dissolve the company and pay off the policyholders with the proceeds. In most states, the rest of the life insurance companies that do business in that State are forced to contribute to a State run guarantee pool. This pool will attempt to make up the difference between what the company has and what it owes. However, there are limits to the coverage provided by these pools. It is very likely in this example that some policyholders will have to forfeit part of the interest that they were promised, and it may take several years for the problem to be resolved satisfactorily. They may even suffer a loss of invested principal.

This is a worst case scenario. In fact, very few life insurance companies fail. By comparison, in the last 10 years, thousands of Banks and Savings & Loan have failed or been taken over by federal regulators. Of course, Banks and Savings & Loans are covered by a guarantee pool that is in turn backed up by the U.S. Government through the Federal Deposit Insurance Corporation (FDIC). Based on their recent history, the Banks and Savings & Loans need the back up.

The point is not that life insurance company fixed annuities are a risky investment from a default standpoint. They have a very low risk of default. The point is that is does happen, and you should pick and choose your life insurance companies carefully. They are not all equally strong or equally prudent. Often, the life insurance company offering the highest interest rates is the one taking the greatest risk.

The second risk with a fixed annuity concerns the nature of making a multi-year, fixed-rate investment. There is the chance that you may need the funds before your term is completed. If so, you will usually have to forfeit some of your interest in the form of "surrender penalties". There is also the risk that the deal you strike today may look like a poor deal next year. This is particularly true if interest rates rise steeply. You may end up averaging 6% for the next 5 years, while interest rates available elsewhere for the next four years might be 8%. Of course, if interest rates fall, you could be a winner.

This sort of "buyers remorse" exists with many other types of investments in which you are getting paid a set amount of interest. For example, bank C.D.s, bonds, and mortgages all can look like poor ideas if rates go up after you buy them, or make you think you're a genius if rates go down after you have locked in your rate.

Finally, over long periods of time, fixed or semi-fixed interest rates such as those found in fixed annuities and Bank C.D.s may not be adequate to keep up with inflation. This is because even though your money may be invested by the bank or insurer in conservative investments that actually outperform inflation in the long run, what you receive is the return that the banks or life insurance companies pay out after they have taken their share. As was mentioned earlier, banks and life insurance companies usually want to make 2% to 3% on the spread. After deducting this fairly high expense, it is tough to beat inflation.

The risks are completely different with the variable annuity. A variable annuity is like a mutual fund. The money invested in a variable annuity is actually kept separate from the general assets of the life insurance company. If the company becomes insolvent, the assets that belong to the variable annuity policyholders will be unaffected. Of course, it would be very inconvenient if the life insurance company running your variable annuity became insolvent, even if it was not a financial problem. You would prefer that a strong company is in charge of your variable annuity.

However, like a mutual fund, the value of your variable annuity will fluctuate based on the value of the stocks or bonds that the various funds purchase. If you invest money into a variable annuity and choose to have all the money put into a blue chip stock mutual fund, the value of your investment will depend on the value of the stocks the fund owns. That value may go up, and sometimes it may go down.

IS THE INSURANCE COMPANY MY FRIEND OR MY ENEMY?

I mentioned earlier that you must treat all investment firms just like any other businesses. The choice of your life insurance company is no different than your choice of long distance telephone service; you have to weigh both cost and quality. Your exact relationship with your life insurance company depends on the type of annuity you purchase.

When you purchase a fixed annuity, you and the life insurance company are sitting on opposite sides of the negotiating table. The more interest they pay you, the less money they make. The less interest they pay you, the more money they make. In addition, they want to tie your money up with them for a long period of time. Partly this is because it makes it easier for them to "match" the term of deposits with investments. Also, it is because it is a lot of work getting new customers. Once they have you, they would prefer it if you would stay with them for a long time.

You are looking to get the best deal for yourself. All things considered, you would like higher interest rates, less time restrictions, and still have the life insurance company invest the money conservatively. The life insurance company would prefer to pay you less, tie your money up for long periods of time, and invest the money to make themselves a lot of money. You can see why you will want to shop around if you are going to use a fixed annuity.

Your relationship with the life insurance company is different if you have a variable annuity. In this case, you are both sitting on the same side of the table. In buying their policy, you have agreed to pay the life insurance company a certain annual percentage to manage the money in the mutual funds. They will go out and invest the money according to the fund's goals and restrictions. In a sense, they are your employee. It is in their best interest to do a good job. The better job they do, the bigger your account grows. The bigger your account, the larger the pool of money that they get paid to manage.

However, not all life insurance companies charge the same to manage variable annuities. Some might charge you a total of 1% a year, while another charges 3% a year. You would prefer to pay your "employees" less to do the same job. They also do not all have similar track records. Although you and the life insurance company are largely on the same side when it comes to this arrangement, it still pays to shop around.

One question that arises is what if the life insurance company is a "mutual" insurance company? A mutual insurance company is one that is not owned by shareholders. Instead, it is owned, technically, by the policy owners themselves and is similar to a life insurance company version of a credit union. Many of the largest life insurance companies in the United States are mutuals. In this case, you may wonder if it is a better deal as you are, in a sense, an owner. The answer is no. You should examine a contract from a mutual exactly as you would examine a contract from any other life insurer. Some of the mutuals will give you a better deal then average, and some will give you a worse deal.

The actual value to you as an individual of this mutual ownership is essentially zero. With a credit union, the member/owners may number a few thousand people who all live in the same area or work for the same employer. Many members are active in choosing who will manage the credit union, and pay attention to issues of costs, interest rates, and service. A mutual life insurance company may have millions of policy owners spread out across the United States. Furthermore, almost none of them actually vote when it comes time to pick who runs the company. The management can run the company as they see fit, and they do not need to necessarily give the policy holders a break on their policies compared to a non-mutual insurance company.

A special mention should be made here about one particular mutual life insurance company. Teachers Insurance and Annuity Association-College Retirement Equities Fund, known as TIAA-CREF, is a very large mutual life insurance company that handles a large part of the 403(b) market. TIAA is the fixed annuity division of the company, while CREF is the variable annuity division. Their annuities are most frequently found being offered in the college and university sector of the 403(b) market. TTIAA-CREF has gained a good reputation of offering low-cost fixed and variable annuity contracts to the 403(b) market.

A second question comes up when you belong to an organization that has made some special arrangement with a particular insurance company. For example, a nationwide teachers organization may sign a deal with ABC Life Insurance Company to provide a "special" policy to its members. This may mean that you will actually be offered a better deal then average by this life insurance company. However, if the leadership of your organization fails to do their homework, you may find out that the deal has no special features or savings compared to what you could find on your own. You will need to examine such a deal as carefully as any other and not get swayed by the marketing appeal of this connection with your member organization.

WHO DOES MY INSURANCE AGENT WORK FOR?

This may come as a surprise to you, but your local life insurance agent does not work for you. They are not, in any legal or practical sense, *your* agent. He or she is an agent of the life insurance company. Even if he or she is an "independent" insurance agent, that only means that he or she works for more than one insurance company.

Insurance agents are paid to sell insurance to people. They are usually paid on a commission system, like stock brokers and real estate agents. If you do not buy a policy from them, they do not make any money. It is in their best interest for you to buy a policy, even if you might not need one or if it is not a very competitive policy. This is not to say that insurance agents are dishonest or unethical. Most are not. However, there is an inherent conflict between what is in your best interest and what is in their best interest. This conflict is the same if you are buying your annuity from a bank or stockbrokerage firm.

Insurance companies know that one of the best ways to motivate agents to sell their policies is to pay higher than normal commissions on the policy. Where does the money come from to pay these higher commissions? From you, of course. Policies that pay more usually have higher annual expenses, or lock you in for more years, or pay you less interest over time. That is how the insurance companies can afford to give the agent more money.

HOW DOES THE SALES CHARGE WORK?

Most fixed and variable annuities involve an life insurance agent being paid to sell you the policy. An agent may receive 5%-8% of every invested dollar as his or her commission. So if you invest $4,000 a year into a 403(b) for 25 years, he or she will collect $5,000-$8,000 in sales commissions. The sales commissions are paid to the agent by the life insurance company. Where does the life insurance company get the money? From you. Here is how it works.

You buy an annuity from ABC Life Insurance Company. You may buy it from one of their own agent/employees. You may buy it from an independent agent. You may even buy it from a bank or brokerage firm if they have a life insurance license. It doesn't really matter. To make the example simple, let's say you give them a lump sum of $10,000 for this annuity. The agent will collect $500 as a sales commission from the life insurance company. The life insurance company now needs to recoup this money from you.

At the time you give them the money, bank C.D. rates are 5%. The interest rate on a medium-term, 10-year U.S. Government bond is 8%. If the life insurance company pays you 6%, they will earn 2% a year on the difference. But because they already paid out 5% to the agent, they need to keep you locked into this arrangement for a number of years to earn back that costs, plus a profit for themselves. So the contract states that if you pull your money out before 7 years are up, you will have to forfeit some of your interest. The amount you lose is called a "surrender charge".

A typical arrangement would say that you will forfeit up to 7% the first year, 6% the second year, 5% the third year, 4% the fourth year, 3% the fifth year, 2% the sixth year, 1% the seventh year. Withdrawals after that year will not be charged. From the standpoint of the life insurance company, once you have bought the annuity, there is no way they can lose out on the sales commission they paid to the agent. If you stay in the annuity for eight years, they make 2% a year for eight years, minus the sales commission (8 years x 2% =16% -5% = 9%). But if you leave sooner than eight years, they get to take back some of the interest they paid you. Most policies will allow you to withdraw some of your money, usually 10% each year, without having to pay the surrender charge. Withdrawals beyond that face the surrender charge.

There is actually one way the life insurance company can lose. If you die after you buy the annuity, your beneficiaries get the principal plus interest, without a surrender charge. So it is possible that the life insurance company could be out the sales commission. They frequently guard against this by making the insurance agent give back the commission if you die within 12 months.

Generally speaking, the more a life insurance company pays out in commissions, the more they must earn from you. So policies that pay high commissions to the agent are usually a worse deal for the investor. However, the amount of the commission paid to the insurance agent is not usually disclosed to you, although you can ask. In fact, in some States, the agent may legally rebate part of the sales commission back to you. In other States, such a practice would be illegal.

Aside from comparing commission levels, it is very difficult to measure the "cost" of one fixed annuity against another fixed annuity. Two life insurance companies can take the same deposit and invest it in the same types of assets, but one may pay you less over time than the other. Or one will start off paying you more in the early years, but pay you less later on. Life insurance companies can offer you a bewildering range of different versions of their fixed annuity, all just a little bit different, and they may change the versions frequently. Many observers believe that life insurance companies do this just to make it difficult to compare.

Even trying to measure annuities by their surrender charges can be difficult. Some may lock you in for seven years with a declining scale of surrender penalties of 7% the first year, 6% the second, 5%, 4%, 3%, 2%, 1%. Another may lock you in for seven years with a surrender penalty of 7% for all seven years. So it is not easy to compare one policy to another, as they are usually not identical.

EVALUATING FIXED ANNUITIES

Most of your decision making when buying a fixed annuity is not designed to let you buy an annuity that will be better than the rest. The fact is, unless you have a crystal ball, there is no way of knowing which fixed annuity will pay you the most interest over the next 10 years. What you are trying to do is avoid buying one that will be worse than average.

When choosing among life insurance companies for a fixed annuity, there are three factors you should examine. One is the financial stability of the life insurance company. The second is the interest rates that you may receive. The third is the liquidity or withdrawal restrictions of the particular annuity contract.

Fixed annuities are basically a deposit made with an insurance company. What you own is the insurance company's promise to pay you your principal plus accumulated interest. So when choosing a life insurance company for an annuity, the first thing you must do is make sure that the life insurance company is financially strong. It is no good getting great terms for your fixed annuity if the life insurance company is going to be unable to make good on its promise.

To be quite honest, it would be very difficult for the layperson to make an informed judgment about the financial strength of any insurance company. It would require a great deal of accounting information and knowledge of the company's investment and operating procedures to be able to arrive at a valid conclusions. Fortunately, there is a simple solution to this problem. Almost all large life insurance companies are rated by outside, independent credit rating agencies. These rating agencies evaluate all of the accounting data and review the company's investment and operating procedures. They then write up a report and assign a rating, usually on some sort of A,B,C or AAA, AA, A scale, that gives you an idea of the strength of the life insurance company. These reports are updated frequently, usually annually. The most recognized firms that rate life insurance companies are A.M. Best & Co., Moodys, and Standard & Poor's.

When you are considering a fixed annuity from a life insurance company, you should always ask the company, or the agent, if they have received a rating from one of the firms mentioned above. Most should have a report from one or more. You should try to get a copy of the report, or at the very least find out the rating assigned. Most life insurance companies can get you a up-to-date copy of the report if you ask for it. Even if you don't understand the entire report, you should still look it over to see if it raises any red flags in your mind.

In general, you should only use a life insurance company who's rating is in the top two categories. For example, AAA or AA from Standard & Poor, or A+ or A from A.M. Best. Whatever advantage you might get from a lower rated life insurance company's fixed annuity contract is unlikely to be worth the extra risk that the company will default.

Once you are using a particular life insurance company, you should check back up on it periodically. Ratings do change, and a company's financial status can decline. If that does happen, you may have to make a decision about pulling your money out, even if that may trigger a surrender penalty, rather than risk having your company go into receivership. Also, please bear in mind that the rating agencies are professional analysts, but they are not fortune tellers. Companies with high ratings can and do go into receivership, sometimes with little or no warning. The financial world moves at an ever increasing pace, and sometimes the rating agencies catch a problem after it is too late.

Because of the risk of default, you may wish to avoid placing too much money into a fixed annuity with any single life insurance company. How much is "too much"? This is hard to say, but many state-run life insurance guarantee pools limit annuity policy protection to $100,000. You may wish to not exceed that amount in fixed annuities with any single life insurance company. If you are using a variable annuity or mutual fund, you do not have the same default concern. There is no real limit to the amount that you hold in a fund, as long as you are satisfied with your overall asset allocation.

A point should be made here about certain attributes used to sell life insurance companies. Many life insurance agents will push a company on you by telling you that *"it's over 50 years or 100 years old"*, or *"it's the largest or ninth largest life insurance company in America"*, or *"it's very well known"*. All of those reasons are interesting, but none of them have any real value to you as an investor. Large, old, and well known life insurance companies can go out of business just like new, small and obscure ones. Neither age, size, or name recognition have any inherent impact on a company's financial soundness. Arguments to use a company based on those reasons are without merit.

Assuming that you are satisfied with the financial soundness of the life insurance company, you now need to consider the specifics of the fixed annuity that you are being offered, including the interest rate you may receive. You want the best deal you can get. There are three things to look at in this stage. You will want to consider the current rate that you are being offered, the minimum rate stated in the contact, and you should try to get the past history of rate changes on that policy.

The existing rate may only be good on the money going into the annuity right now. Furthermore, it may only last for one year. So you should not get too excited by whatever rate you are quoted unless it is guaranteed for a number of years. In fact, if the rate is noticeably higher than what you are being quoted by other companies, you should be wary. If you are locked in for seven or eight years by surrender charges, they have plenty of time to offset their generous first year rate by giving you lower renewal rate.

The minimum guaranteed rate is usually going to be somewhere around 4%-5%. You may never actually be paid that rate. On the other hand, if you keep a policy long enough, interest rates are bound to swing up and down. Sooner or later they may get down to your minimum.

The life insurance company or a good insurance agent should be able to show you the history of renewal interest rates that the company has paid on policies AFTER the initial rate guarantee has expired. This gives you a good idea of how fairly the insurer has dealt with their policy holders. The company cannot control what happens to interest rates in the future, but they can make an attempt to remain competitive in any case. If you are comparing two insurance annuities side-by-side, this information can be very revealing. If one firm has a tendency to offer teaser rates, and then drop the rate quickly in later years, it will show up in the comparison. You should always ask the life insurance company or agent for this information. You may also want to get from another source, such as a financial magazine, a chart showing other types of interest rates over the same time period. For example, a chart showing the movement of interest rates on Treasury Bills or bank C.D.s over the last 5 years. You may notice that most life insurance companies, like most banks, tend to be quicker to lower rates on deposits when prevailing rates fall than they are to raise them when rates move up.

Finally, there is the issue of liquidity. How restricted are you by the terms of the contract from pulling your money out? The best deal, and the rarest, is finding a fixed annuity contract with no surrender charges at all. Except for some variable annuity contracts that are a combined effort between a no-load mutual fund group and a life insurance company, "no-load" fixed and variable annuities are uncommon. If you work for a very large employer, they might be able to negotiate such a deal, but generally speaking, you will be facing surrender charges.

Most contracts will allow you to withdraw up to 10% a year from your contract without triggering surrender charges. Beyond that, surrender charges might extend anywhere from 5 to 12 years. It is in your best interest to have the shortest period possible, both because you might want to spend or move the money, and because it forces the life insurance company to remain competitive.

You should also look to see if a policy contains a "bail-out" provision which would allow you to move the money, without surrender charge, if the rate they pay you drops below a set level. For example, the policy might pay you 8% the first year and have surrender penalties extending out 6 years, but the bail-out provision would allow you to keep or move the funds, without surrender charge, if the new rate ("renewal rate") is ever below 7%. A fixed annuity policy with a bail-out feature and a 5 year or less surrender period would be a fairly liquid contract, while surrender charges of more than 7 years, and no bail-out, would be considered restrictive.

There are two special types of fixed annuities that you should be wary of if offered. The first some times is called a "two-tiered" annuity. In this annuity, you are paid higher interest rate than most other fixed annuities. However, if you ever surrender the policy, you receive a lower interest rate. So the policy ends up always having two cash values, or tiers. The first is the value if you keep the policy. The second is the value if you surrender the policy. So you may have a policy in which the first tier cash value is $100,000, but the second tier cash value is $85,000. You can take out up to 10% a year out without affecting the interest rate. You may also "annuitize" based on the higher cash value. That is you may exchange the deferred annuity for an immediate annuity that will pay you a monthly check for the rest of your life. Or your beneficiary may receive the higher value at your death.

Essentially, you have a policy that has surrender charges that never go away. What is worse, the higher cash value figure is, for all intents and purposes, a fiction. You will probably never live to see it. If you annuitize, the life insurance company gets to pick the "internal rate of return" (see Chapter 11). So even though they will base your monthly payments on the higher value, they can select a low interest rate when making the calculations. The result is that you may end up receiving the same amount in a monthly check as if you had annuitized the smaller amount with a more competitive life insurance company. Using the 10% a year method could mean that it may take the rest of your life to get the money out. And, of course, the third method requires you to die.

A second tricky fixed annuity version is one in which you are offered an above average deal, usually a better interest rate. However, if you get out within a set period of time, the life insurance company gets to make a "market adjustment" to the value of the account. If interest rates have gone up, your cash value will be adjusted down, and vice-a-versa. There are usually limits to the potential adjustments. In essence, the life insurance company is making you shoulder part of the market risk on the bonds they buy.

The life insurance company usually buys bonds with your annuity deposits. The average term of the bonds is matched against the expected average term of the annuity deposits. This reduces the likelihood that the life insurance company will be forced to sell bonds early. If too many people leave early, the insurance company has to sell bonds early to get cash to pay them off. Those bonds may sell for more, or less, than what the life insurance company paid for them. Normally, any loss is borne by the life insurance company. This is part of the reason they like to earn so much more on the deposits than they pay out, to help cushion possible losses.

But on these market adjusted annuities, they essentially let they people who cash out receive most of the loss, or gain, from the sale of the bonds. In exchange, they tend to pay them a higher interest rate than a conventional policy. Think carefully before you select one of these fixed annuities. If you get out early, you may find yourself in a situation similar to one if you had bought a bond mutual fund that fluctuates in value. After all, the primary reason you buy a fixed annuity in which the life insurance company is just going to buy bonds with the money is because the life insurance company accepts the market risk, and so the value of your principal is stable. If the principal value isn't going to be stable, you might as well use your 403(b) to buy a low-cost bond fund and cut out the life insurance company expense entirely.

As was mentioned, what you are attempting to do is eliminate the bad choices, not find the one that will turn out 10 years from now to have been the best choice. If after doing your evaluation you are still left with several choices that you are satisfied with, than go ahead and select the one you feel most comfortable with at the time. Nobody, including the life insurance companies, can tell ahead of time whether your choice is the optimal selection. But if you are satisfied with it, that is all that matters.

Measuring costs on variable annuities is much easier. Most variable annuities also pay the insurance agent a sales commission. For that reason, they will also usually lock you in for 5-7 years with a surrender charge, just like the fixed annuity. But variable annuities will also tell you exactly how much your annual costs are for the policy. You will find that information in the policy contract or disclosure statement. These costs can be used to compare two different variable annuities.

The annual cost of a variable annuity is the total of three different figures. The first is what the life insurance company charges for the annuity expenses. This may be referred to as mortality charges and this is what the life insurance company is paid for providing the annuity. It might be a figure like 1% annually. If you keep reading the disclosure statement, you will find a second listing for the actual charge for running the mutual funds within the annuity. This cost might be another 1% - 1.5% annually. Finally, you may have a fixed annual account or contract charge of $30 a year. Your expenses are the total of these figures.

Variable annuities used as 403(b)s investments charge an average of just over 2% a year. They also lock you in for 6 to 7 years on average. However, some have even higher charges or longer surrender periods. In many cases, this is because they pay above average sales commissions to the insurance agents. You will want to avoid these plans.

On the other hand, some variable annuities may be bought "no-load". That is to say they are sold directly to you by the life insurance company, without going through an agent. They are also sold without any sales commissions being paid. These no-load annuities are often offered by a life insurance company in partnership with a no-load mutual fund family. Since the life insurance company does not have to earn back a sales commission, they don't need to charge you as much each year, or lock you in for a period of years. No-load variable annuities might charge you half as much annually as other variable annuities, and have no surrender charges. All other things being equal, they are a better deal for you. They are however, not a very good deal for your insurance agent or stockbroker. If you want to find such a no-load variable annuity, you will have to seek it out yourself, the agents have no incentive to help you find one. Some companies that offer such no-load variable annuities include Vanguard Funds, Scudder Funds, and Charles Schwab & Co.

CHAPTER SEVEN

MUTUAL FUNDS

The other provider of investments to the 403(b) market is the mutual fund industry. It is very likely that they will become increasingly active in this area. Over the last 20 years, mutual funds have become the dominant investment tool for the American populace to use for their financial planning. But even people who own mutual funds outside of their 403(b) plan still don't know how they really work. The points to understand include:

* **WHAT IS A MUTUAL FUND?**

* **HOW ARE THEY ORGANIZED?**

* **LOAD VERSUS NO-LOAD**

* **HOW ARE EXPENSES CHARGED?**

* **WHAT VARIETIES ARE THERE?**

* **WHAT ARE THE RISKS OF THE VARIOUS TYPES?**

* **HOW TO EVALUATE AND SELECT FUNDS**

As the book will make clear, mutual funds are generally the best investment vehicle for 403(b)s, and likely to be the dominant choice in the future. It is essential that anyone planning their financial future understand how mutual fund's function.

WHAT IS A MUTUAL FUND?

A mutual fund is a method of investing into various types of securities such as stocks or bonds. A fund is merely a vehicle for making the investments; it is not really the investments themselves. In this sense, a mutual fund is a financial intermediary, like a bank or a life insurance company. All of these intermediaries take your money and turn around and invest it in various types of securities, investments, or loans. There is one major difference, however, between a bank or a life insurance company and a mutual fund. The depositors at a bank do not own the bank or its assets. The investors ("shareholders") in a mutual fund DO own the mutual fund and all of its financial assets.

As we saw in the last chapter, depositing money with a bank or in a fixed annuity at a life insurance company is really a form of a loan made by you to the financial firm. The bank or the life insurance company invests the money for more than they pay you, and keep the difference. In a mutual fund, you and the other shareholders own the assets and reap all of the benefits. You also bear all of the risks. Variable annuities are essentially mutual funds run by life insurance companies, so most of this chapter applies to variable annuities as well.

HOW ARE THEY ORGANIZED?

Mutual funds are organized along similar lines. The general shape of mutual funds is largely influenced by the regulations of the Security and Exchange Commission (S.E.C.), the I.R.S., and industry practices.

As an example, let us say that there is a mutual fund that was designed to invest in U.S. Government bonds. We will call it the "Fund". When the Fund was originally set up and registered with the S.E.C., a document called a prospectus was written. The prospectus is a legally binding description of the Fund, including its goals and investment restrictions.

In this example, the prospectus states that the Fund's primary investment goal is to generate income. The Fund also seeks to avoid principal losses due to defaults on bonds, and will only buy bonds issued or guaranteed by the U.S. Government. You will be able to purchase or redeem the Fund's shares on a daily basis (an "open-ended" mutual fund). Finally, the prospectus will detail the expenses and charges of the Fund.

The Fund is already in existence, so we will say that there are 20,000 existing shareholders. There are currently 10,000,000 shares of the Fund outstanding, and the value of the Fund's total assets is currently $120,000,000. The value of each share is $12 ($120 million divided by 10 million shares). This price is called the Net Asset Value ("NAV"). When an investor wishes to buy new shares, he pays the NAV, plus any sales charge ("load"). If a shareholder wishes to sell shares, they sell them at the NAV (some funds have a sales charge when you sell). Variable annuities don't call their ownership units "shares". They usually call them "accumulation units", although there is no real difference between the two concepts.

The $120 million in assets is composed of various U.S. Government securities and cash. Each business day, the Fund will calculate the current market value of the assets, based on the prices of the securities at the close of the market (usually 4:00 p.m. EST) . As the value of the investments go up and down, so does the Net Asset Value. All of that money belongs to the shareholders. If the Fund decided to go out of business tomorrow, the shareholders would split up the assets on a per share basis. The breakup value of the Fund and its N.A.V. should be the same.

Most funds are organized as corporations or as business trusts. They are run by a Board of Directors or a Board of Trustees. The Board is usually elected by the shareholders, although the prospectus may not call for regular elections. The Board hires a firm to act as the Fund's "Manager". The Manager takes care of making the day-to-day investment decisions, as well as the record-keeping. When you call a mutual fund, you are actually dealing with the Fund Managers. In a sense, they are hired hands employed by the shareholders to run the Fund. The Fund Managers do not own the Fund, the shareholders do.

To avoid potential problems, the Fund Managers do not physically control the cash and investments of the Fund. The Board hires a "Custodian" to guard the assets. The Custodian is usually a bank or trust company. This role of custodian is different from the role of a 403(b)7 custodian discussed in earlier chapters. When money is sent to the Fund to buy new shares, the money actually goes to the Fund's Custodian. They tell the Fund Managers how much cash is available every morning. The Managers can then use the new cash to purchase more investments and inform the Custodian of their action. The Custodian will pay the seller of the investments, usually a brokerage firm, and in return the Custodian will receive the stock or bond certificates. The investments are registered in the name of the Fund. When money is withdrawn from the Fund, the reverse occurs. This dual control arrangement makes it very difficult for anyone to embezzle money from the Fund.

The Board of the Fund also will hire an outside firm of C.P.A.s to audit the books and produce the annual report. In addition, they employ a law firm to be the Fund's lawyers.

HOW DO THEY FUNCTION?

Most mutual funds are part of "families". A family of funds is one in which a number of funds share a common Fund Manager and Custodian. They may also share the same set of lawyers, C.P.A.s, and membership on the Board of Directors. The funds may have similar sounding names, for example the "ABC Government Bond Fund" and the "ABC Stock Fund". Variable annuities are a family run by a life insurance company. A family of funds may have anywhere from four or five funds to a hundred or more. Some of the well known mutual fund families include Fidelity, Vanguard, Scudder, Putnam and Franklin.

It may sound as if the Fund Managers are just hired by the Board to perform a service. In reality, most mutual funds are originally set up by the Fund Management company itself. They will usually pay the start-up expenses, as well as the initial cost of marketing the Fund to investors. They also retain seats on the Board of the Fund, and make sure that any of the "independent" directors are favorably disposed towards the management firm. The Managers hope the Fund becomes large enough so that they can make a living off being the managers. Although the Fund belongs to the shareholders, they are mostly run by the Fund Managers. Rarely does a Board act to fire the management group and replace them with another manager, although it does happen.

A mutual fund management company has three main tasks. The first is the job of investment management. Certain individuals or committees are in charge of managing the Fund's portfolio and following the guidelines of the prospectus and the Board. Beyond that, they are largely free to use their own judgment as to how they will invest the assets.

The second part of the job is the record-keeping and accounting function. If the Fund has 20,000 shareholders, someone must keep track of them and send them statements. Statements are usually sent monthly or quarterly. Tax statements must be sent out at year's end. The Custodian must be told to process checks based on purchases and sales. This record keeping function is sometimes called the "transfer agency". The accounting functions are quite complex. The figures must be examined from the Custodian and the CPA firm to make sure they balance. An entire range of SEC and IRS rules and filings must also be followed. Finally, every year the Fund must send out its annual report, as well as update the prospectus. Some mutual fund families have all of these services performed by the Fund Management company. However, other fund groups hire a separate company to perform the transfer agency.

The last area is that of sales and marketing. It won't do the Fund Managers any good if they have a fund and a staff, but no shareholders and no assets to manage. Although everyone loves to talk about the portfolio managers and the Fund's past performance, it is mostly because of marketing that small funds become big funds.

Mutual funds are sold two ways. The first is by stockbrokers and others selling a fund to you. The broker, bank, or insurance agent acts as a middleman in much the same way as a clothing retailer acts as a middleman between you and the clothing manufacturer. This is very similar to the way most life insurance and annuities are sold. The second method is by having interested investors buy the Fund directly from the Fund family. From the investors standpoint, the main difference between the two methods involves sales charges.

LOAD VERSUS NO-LOAD

If a Fund family sells shares directly to the public without a middlemen, the Fund is also usually sold without any sales charge (think of it as buying clothes wholesale from the manufacturer). This arrangement is called a "No-Load" mutual fund. There are also no-load variable annuities. The Fund managers usually rely on mass advertising, past performance, and word of mouth to attract buyers. The buyers call the Fund family up and are sent a prospectus and an account form. They return the form with their check, and purchase their shares at Net Asset Value (NAV). The portfolio managers puts the money to work, and the record keepers start sending statements to the owner. When an investor wants to sell, they contact the Fund family. The Fund liquidates their shares at NAV and sends them the money.

When you buy shares in a Fund that uses a middleman/retail arrangement as their primary marketing channel, a sales charge is usually levied. For example, you talk to a stockbroker, insurance agent, or the investment salesman down at the bank who recommends a certain mutual fund to you. You give him your check for $10,000. At this point, one of two arrangements usually occurs.

In the first, called a "front-load", the broker sends the money to the Fund. You buy your shares at NAV plus a markup which typically runs

4%-6% (by law, it cannot exceed 8.5%). So of your $10,000, perhaps only $9,600 goes to buying shares. The other $400 is paid to the brokerage firm as a sales commission. When you sell your shares, you get the NAV. So if you bought today and sold tomorrow, you would be out the 4% commission.

As you can imagine, this does not appeal to many people. So the mutual fund industry borrowed an idea from the life insurance industry. This is the "back end-load". When you invest, you purchase your shares at NAV. The Fund family still pays the salesman his or her 4% sales commission. However, you are now locked in for 5 or 6 years. If you sell before then, you pay a sales charge when you leave. Furthermore, the annual expenses on back end-loaded funds are higher than on an identical front-load fund. For example, if the total operating expenses of a front-load mutual fund cost 1% a year, the annual expenses on an identical back end-load fund might be 1 1/2% - 2%. So if you stay for the 5 years or longer, they collect the sales charge back in the form of higher annual expenses. If you leave early, they get it as a "contingent deferred sales charge". No matter what you do, you are going to pay them their money. If this sounds just like the way most life insurance and annuity policies are sold, it should. That's where the mutual fund industry got the idea.

In a fairly new development, some load mutual fund families sell shares in a single mutual fund BOTH ways. You can buy shares and pay a front-load, or you can buy them with the back end-load and higher annual expenses. The mutual fund usually calls the front-load shares "A Class Shares", and the back end-load shares "B Class Shares", but both classes of shares are for the exact same mutual fund. The marketing people at load mutual funds are working on even more share class types in which they continue to juggle front-load charges, back end-load charges, and annual expenses to produce different variety of shares in the same fund.

In the long run, a back end-loaded mutual fund will usually end up costing you more for sales expenses than a similar front-end loaded fund. This is because the front-end load is a one time charge, while the higher expenses of a back-end loaded fund may go on forever. If you invested $10,000 into a stock mutual fund with a 4% front-load, you will pay $400 as a sales charge once. If you bought it as a back end-leaded fund, it might cost you an extra 1/2% - 1% for as long as you have the fund, plus you pay the higher annual expense on your entire account balance, not just the initial investment. So if the value of your account grows over time, so does the cost of the higher expenses.

A common question is which type of fund has better investment performance, load funds or no-load funds? The answer is that, if you ignore the negative effect on an investment of the sales charges, there is no difference between the performance of no-load funds compared to load funds. Sales charges aside, the average load fund and the average no-load fund do about the same. Some funds do better than average, and some do worse, but it has nothing to do with the type of sales arrangement. If you factor the sales charge in, as a real investor must, the advantage swings to the no-load. A no-load investor either saves 4%-6% up front compared to the front-load investor; or saves 1/2% to 1% a year in expenses compared to the back end-load mutual fund.

In an attempt to defend the cost of the sales commissions, many salesmen will trot out a load fund which has greatly outperformed the average no-load. They will use this as "proof" that it is worth paying a load for a fund because this fund's track record is so good. What they don't mention is that you could just as easily go out and find a similar no-load fund with an above average track record. After all, if you have 100 load funds and 100 no-load funds of a particular investment style, the top ten of each would be quite a bit better than average. But the no-loads would still be cheaper to buy, and therefore, a better deal for the investor. Many salespeople will tell you that load funds as a group have better performance than no-loads. This is an untrue statement. They may also tell you that no-load funds have higher annual operating costs than load funds. That is also an untrue statement. Most surveys have shown that the annual operating costs of no-load funds as a group is less than the annual operating costs of load funds. Furthermore, the annual costs of both types of funds are less then the average annual cost of variable annuities.

In fact, you may take the issue of load versus no-load performance one step further. Studies have been conducted by various investment firms and financial magazines to try and see if there is ANY positive relationship between paying higher expenses or sales charges and getting better performance. The conclusions have shown that the more you spend on investment expenses, the LESS likely you are to have better than average performance.

The question arises as to why you would pay extra for a load fund? The answer is that you do not buy a load fund to get better performance. You buy a load fund to get the advice and help of the salesperson from whom you bought the investment. He or she should have helped you make certain financial planning decisions, and also helped select the best funds to meet your needs. If they do, perhaps they are worth the 4%. On the other hand, many investors don't need or don't get this professional hand-holding. In that case, the sales commission is wasted.

In a sense, load versus no-load it is a bit like the choice you have when you go to the gas station. You can go to a self-serve station, pay less, and pump your own gas. Or you can go to the full service station, pay extra, and have someone else pump your gas. You can't tell, based just on whether a station is full-service or self-service, who has better gasoline. You just know that you can pay someone to do part of the job for you. However, the worse thing to do is to go to the full-service station AND pump your own gas. Likewise, if you are going to research mutual funds yourself and pick them, why would you pay an extra 5% and get a load fund when you will be able to find equally good no-loads?

The decision by the mutual fund managers to be a no-load or load fund is strictly a marketing decision. If they think that they can get brokers to sell their Fund, they will go that route. If they think that they can sell it no-load, they choose that method. From their standpoint, once the money is in the door, it matters little how it got there (similarly, the oil company doesn't really care if its stations are full-serve or self-serve, as long as people buy a lot of their gasoline).

HOW ARE EXPENSES CHARGED?

If no-load funds don't have sales charges, and load funds give the sales charge to the brokers, how do the managers of the Fund make any money? The answer is that ALL mutual funds have "annual expenses" that are paid from the Fund's income and assets. These expenses are the overhead, or cost, of running the Fund.

When you look at a fund's prospectus, it will usually show you on the second page both the sales charges and annual operating expenses of the fund. If it is a no-load, the sales charge columns will show 0%. Otherwise, it will tell you if the sales load is a front-load, or a back end-load ("contingent deferred sales charge").

The expense chart has a total annual figure, reported as a percentage. For example, the total annual expense ratio of our U.S. Government bond Fund might be .60%. That is to say, 6/10 of 1%. This figure will be broken down into three sub-categories. The first is the fund managers fee, the second is the miscellaneous expenses, and the third could be an annual sales expense called a 12b-1 (named after the S.E.C. regulation permitting such charges).

The first expense is the percentage that the Fund Managers are paid by the Board of Directors for running the Fund. From that, they usually pay most of the operating costs of the Fund, such as salaries, advertising, office expenses, and the cost of the shareholder record-keeping (transfer agency). Certain expenses are normally not paid by the Fund Manager. Instead, the Fund itself directly pays for them (for example, certain filing fees, accounting charges, and legal costs). This is the miscellaneous expense figure and is the second figure listed in the prospectus.

On a no-load fund, and many front-loaded funds, the total of these two figures is what the shareholders pay annually for the operation of the Fund. It actually matters little how the expenses are broken down between these two categories. An investor only cares about the total. Like any business, an owner/shareholder would prefer lower overhead. Since the expenses must be paid before the shareholders get their return, high expenses just cut into the shareholder's profits.

The third expense, the 12b-1 fee, occurs in many front-load funds and almost all back end-loaded funds. The Fund Manager uses the money to either pay themselves back for sales commissions that they paid out to brokers, or to actually pay the brokers a small annual commission (called a "trailer"). The rather silly theory behind 12b-1 fees is that they would benefit the existing shareholders by giving the Fund Managers more money to market with, thus allowing the Fund to grow larger. If the Fund was larger, it could spread its fixed expenses over a greater asset base, and lower the annual expense ratio. So you raise annual expenses to lower annual expenses. There is only one problem with that concept. Once a fund introduces a 12b-1 fee, it doesn't usually get rid of it. So expenses go up, but not back down. In any event, despite the claims of the stockbrokers, a 12b-1 fee does not appear to help the existing shareholders.

Many or most mutual fund families charge an annual fee for any retirement account which requires a custodian, such as an IRA or a 403(b)7 account. This charge will usually run anywhere from $10 - $40 per year. Variable annuities frequently have a similar charge, sometimes called a "contract" charge, that also tends to be in the $10 - $40 range.

On a variable annuity, there will be one other expense. This is a charge for the life insurance company itself, above and beyond what you pay for the fund management. This might run 1/2% to 1% annually. Since variable annuities and mutual funds are treated equally under the 403(b) code for tax purposes, this extra level of expense on variables tends to make mutual funds a more attractive choice.

EXPENSE SHEET FROM A PROSPECTUS

	"Front Load"	"Back-Load"	"No-Load"
SHAREHOLDER TRANSACTION EXPENSES			
Sales Charge on Purchases	4.5%	None	None
Sales Charge on Reinvested Dividends	4.5%	None	None
Deferred Sales Charge	None	5%	None
ESTIMATED ANNUAL FUND OPERATING EXPENSES			
Management Fees	.80%	.80%	.80%
12b-1 Fees	None	.50%	None
Other Fees	.20%	.20%	.20%
Total Fund Operating Expenses	1%	1.5%	1%

VARIETIES OF MUTUAL FUNDS/VARIABLE ANNUITIES ARE THERE?

Mutual funds are divided into various types by their goals and investment restrictions. Although there are thousands of mutual funds, the majority of mutual funds and variable annuity funds can be divided into a small number of major categories.

One category is mutual funds that basically take no market risks at all. These funds, called MONEY MARKET FUNDS, only buy short-term, highly rated debt securities. For example, a fund might only buy 90-day Treasury bills from the U.S. Government. There is little real risk of the fund losing money by default. Furthermore, because the investments are so short-term, there is no real change in the value of the investments caused by swings in the market. Money market funds usually have a share price (NAV) of $1 a share, and that figure does not change.

Although money market funds are very secure investments, the returns on them over the long run tends to be low compared to other types of investments. They can only earn as much as the prevailing rate of return on short-term, low risk investments. Although there have been times in the past when short-term, low risk investments have had high returns, over the long run the returns tend to be fairly low. As such, they make only limited sense for a 403(b) account.

The next major category is BOND or FIXED-INCOME FUNDS. These funds invest in debt securities, or IOUs, issued by large borrowers. Unlike the short-term money market funds, these investments may be medium-term or long-term. Bond funds buy bonds, mortgage bonds, and other types of debt to earn the interest that the investments pay them. There is also the possibility of capital gains (or losses) caused by swings in the market value of bonds.

Between the time a bond is first issued and when it comes due and is paid off, the market value of the bond will change. The market value is what that bond is worth if you sold it TODAY. So a bond issued two years ago with a face maturity value of $10,000 due in another five years may have a market value higher or lower than $10,000. The difference depends on the interest rate this bond is paying compared to the current interest rate market. If the current interest rate for five year bonds is 7%, and you have an older bond that matures in five years that is paying 8%, issued at a time when interest rates were higher, your market value is greater. If, however, you have an older bond that is paying 6%, your market value is lower.

Some bond funds, such as those that buy municipal bonds, have no place in a 403(b) because of tax reasons. Because municipal bonds are tax-free, they tend to pay less interest than taxable government or corporate bonds. However, since a 403(b) is tax protected anyway, you would be better off investing in bonds with a higher rate. Beyond that, bond funds come in three major varieties: HIGH QUALITY, LOW QUALITY, and FOREIGN.

High quality bond funds buy bonds from issuers with strong credit ratings. Many buy only U.S. Government securities. Others also buy corporation bonds with high credit ratings, or bonds back by pools of home mortgages (such as GNMAs). With these funds, the risk of loss because an issuer defaults is very low. However, the change in market value because of changes in current interest rates still occurs. It is possible to have gains or losses on your share price.

Low quality bond funds are sometimes called High Yield Funds. They are also called Junk Bond Funds. These funds invest in bonds from issuers with poor credit ratings. Because of the poor ratings, these bonds usually pay much higher interest rates than high quality bonds. However, the risk of default is also much greater. If things work out, the fund will make more money than the high quality bond fund, because of the higher interest rate. However, because of the greater uncertainty of payments, the market value of junk bonds tend to swing more than the value of high quality bonds. Sometimes these junk bonds do default. You are accepting more risk to earn a greater return.

Foreign bond funds invest in bonds issued overseas. This is because interest rates can be higher in other countries. Managers may also buy bonds from another country because they think its currency will rise against the American dollar. These funds, like junk bond funds, are an attempt to make more money in bonds by taking more risk.

The third major category of mutual funds is STOCK or EQUITY FUNDS. These funds invest primarily in the common stock of corporations. Unlike bonds, which can represent borrowing by a corporation, stocks represents the actual ownership of the company (equity). A fund that buys stocks makes money because the corporations earn profits and pay dividends, and because the value of the corporation's stock rises. They can be divided into four main varieties: LARGE AMERICAN COMPANY STOCKS, SMALL AMERICAN COMPANY STOCKS, FOREIGN COMPANY STOCKS and SPECIALTY STOCK FUNDS.

Many funds focus on the stocks of large American corporations. These companies tend to be the giants of their industry. As a group, large companies' stock prices have historically tended to grow more slowly and with less volatility than smaller companies' stocks. These funds are often labeled "GROWTH & INCOME" funds.

Those interested in more potential return and who are willing to live with more risk often invest in the stocks of smaller American companies. These types of mutual funds are often labeled "GROWTH" or "AGGRESSIVE GROWTH" funds.

Foreign Stock funds attempt to make their returns buying the stocks of non-American companies. They may make money because a foreign company is growing faster than similar American firms, or because a foreign stock market is rising faster than the U.S. market, or because the foreign currency rises against the American dollar. In any event, these funds take a greater risk and seek greater returns than most American-only stock funds.

In addition to the main categories above, there are a number of Specialty Funds. These funds may invest in a single industry, such as biotechnology. They may invest in only certain types of situations, like stocks of companies facing takeovers. As a general rule, most specialty stock funds are a higher return/ higher risk proposition than the typical, broadly diversified stock fund.

One type of Specialty Fund bears a closer look. This is the INDEX FUND. An index fund is a stock or bond fund that elects to dispense with the services of a portfolio manager and instead employs a fairly simple buy and hold strategy. For example, the Fund may just go out and buy all of the stocks that are part of a market index.

A market index is a group of stocks, or bonds, whose price movement is used as a means of measuring the movement of a market as a whole. For example, the Dow Jones Industrial Average is composed of 30 large company's stocks and their prices. It is the oldest market index. When people say that "the market is up today", they often mean that the Dow Jones 30 is up. Most investment professionals actually pay more attention to the Standard & Poor's 500 Index ("S&P500"). Although it is not as old as the Dow Jones Index, it includes a much larger and more representative group of companies, and is thought to be a much more accurate gauge of the American stock market than the Dow Jones.

An Index Fund might go out and invest a percentage in all 500 company stocks in the S&P 500. It would then simply hold on to those stocks, as long as the company's stock remains part of the S&P 500. This type of investing is sometimes referred to as "passive" portfolio management. As a result, the return of the Index Fund will tend to be the same as the return on the actual index. The Fund Manager will not need to employ a team of portfolio managers and analysts, since the Fund is not really engaging in any stock selection process at all. An Index Fund can have annual expenses that are much lower than other, actively managed mutual funds. So while a typical American stock fund might have annual expenses of 1.25%, a stock index fund might have expenses as low as 0.25%. In addition, the Index Fund does not incur as much cost trading stocks back and forth, unlike the active fund.

The appeal of Index Funds is simple. By design, an Index Fund cannot really do much worse, or much better, than the average of the market itself as measured by the particular index. In fact, its return should be equal to the return of the index itself, minus the Index Fund's annual expenses. This may not sound like such a great deal until you find out the majority of stock mutual funds fail to do that well themselves. Because of their much higher annual expenses and the trading costs they incur by frequently buying and selling stocks, about two thirds of actively managed American stock funds fail to equal or surpass the return of the market over time. When you buy an actively managed fund, you are doing so in the hope that the manager will be able to be one of the one third who might beat the market over time. The odds are not in your favor. If you buy an Index Fund, you are not trying to beat the market, but you also don't have to worry about being part of the majority of funds that will underperform the market. So the lure of the Index Fund is simple. You give up the chance of having your fund be the top performing fund, but you also give up the bigger risk that your fund will be part of the majority of funds that fail to outperform the market.

Finally, there are two types of funds that represent mixtures of the other categories. A BALANCE FUND is a fund that is a semi-permanent mixture of stocks and bonds. For example, it might always be about 50% bonds and 50% stocks. Investing $10,000 in a balanced fund might be similar to owning $5,000 in a stock fund and $5,000 in a bond fund. This type of fund tends to be a fairly conservative selection for an investor, because the assets are so broadly diversified.

An ASSET ALLOCATION FUND is a fund that mixes stock, bond, money market, and foreign stock all in one fund. But unlike the balanced fund, the asset allocation fund frequently changes the mixture in an attempt to catch the next "hot" market. So if the manager thinks that bonds will outperform American stocks over the next 12 months, he or she will reduce the percentage of holdings in stocks and increase the percentage in bonds. Asset allocation funds, like many of the specialty funds, are a fairly new concept. It remains to be seen if they work as well as their proponents claim.

MUTUAL FUNDS: FRIEND OR FOE?

Like the variable annuity, when you deal with a mutual funds, you are the owner. You and the managers of the funds sit on the same side of the table. It is everyone's desire that the fund do well. You care because it is your money. The fund managers care because they get paid a percentage of the assets. However, you must always bear in mind that the annual expenses charged by managers vary enormously. It is in your best interest to have lower expenses.

The issue of the stockbroker or mutual fund salesperson and his or her commission is different. It is a personal choice based on your view of the value of the advice that you might receive from the broker. For some people, giving 4%-6% of their money to someone for advice may be worthwhile. For others, it is a complete waste of money. You must also bear in mind that while many brokers will do a good job of advising you, many may not. Although they all now tend to have various impressive sounding titles, such as financial consultant, when you get to the heart of the matter, they are salespeople. And like the insurance salespeople, none of them will get paid unless you buy something.

VARIABLE ANNUITIES: SPECIAL FEATURES

There are two special features of variable annuities compared to mutual funds that should be mentioned. The first is that a variable deferred annuity can be converted into an immediate annuity when you retire, a mutual fund cannot. You will remember that an immediate annuity is one which is paying you a periodic payment, like a pension. Of course, you may not want to convert your deferred annuity to an immediate annuity (see Chapter 11). Furthermore, you can always sell your 403(b) mutual funds and buy an immediate annuity if you really want to set one up.

Second, if you die while owning your deferred variable annuity, your heirs will usually get back, at a minimum, the amount you invested, even if the share value of the funds has declined. This is not true of a mutual fund. So if you put $10,000 into a variable annuity, and the funds are only worth $9,000 when you die because the stock market has declined, your heirs still get $10,000 back. If the accounts are worth $15,000, they get the larger amount. In theory, this advantage is part of the reason you end up paying an extra 1% a year in expenses on the average variable annuity compared to the average mutual fund.

However, this is not as valuable a feature as it sounds. It only has value if two things are true, the account value is down and you die. Due to the fact that your variable annuity will probably make money over time, there may not be many instances when this benefit would come into play. It is likely that this will only work out if you put money into an annuity, this year or next year is a down year, and then you die. Remember that if you put in $10,000 today, and the funds are up 10% this year, they will have to drop more than 10% next year, and you have to die, for this feature to be a benefit. So if you have had the policy for a number of years, you are likely to be ahead anyway.

This benefit ends up being a very inefficient and expensive form of life insurance. Inefficient because it only pays off if you die early in the process during a down year. Expensive because you are paying 1% a year to protect your heirs against potential losses that might be -10% or -20% under most worst case scenarios. To be quite honest, you would be better off taking the 1% a year and just buying more straight life insurance coverage. It would pay your heirs regardless of what the annuity account values were, and they would likely receive more money.

70

SELECTING MUTUAL FUNDS AND VARIABLE ANNUITIES

If you are going to pay a stockbroker or insurance agent a sales commission to sell you a mutual fund or variable annuity, you can skip this section. After all, if you are willing to pay them a commission, you might as well make them do the job. If you are not going to pay them a commission, keep reading.

When choosing mutual funds or variable annuities, there are three factors that you must examine. They are not the same three factors used to pick fixed annuities.

The first factor is you want to choose a fund which will match your asset allocation goals. If you decide in your asset allocation to make use of a stock fund that invests mostly in the stocks of large, American corporations, than make sure the fund you select is doing so. Although it sounds elementary, it is amazing how many people invest in funds whose investment style fails to match their own goals. Sometimes this is because the investor heard that the fund was "a good fund" and so they bought it. This can be a bit like going into a car dealership to buy a family sedan and coming out with a pick-up truck. It may be a "great truck", but it is not what you wanted or needed. You should never buy a fund unless it fits your goals and asset allocation needs, even if someone assures you that it is a "great fund".

Another reason that investors buy funds that don't match their needs is that they never bothered to check and see what the fund purchases, or what are its investment goals. In the fund's prospectus, it will usually tell you in the first few pages what the fund does and does not do with your money, and what is the stated investment goal of the fund. If the goal and limitations of the fund do not match what you want, throw the prospectus away and find another fund.

The second area to evaluate when selecting mutual funds or variable annuities is the expenses and charges that the fund shareholders must pay. You must look at both the annual operating costs of the fund, and whether or not there are any sales charges, either front-load or back end-load, involved.

As far as annual expenses are concerned, the lower the better. The more that is spent on annual expenses, the less the shareholders receive. In some types of funds, such as money market funds, the difference between two different money market fund's return over time may be

71

explained entirely by the difference in their annual expense ratios. Even with stock mutual funds, you would just as soon pay less. As a rule of thumb, a low-cost money market fund will have annual expenses of .6 of 1% or less. A low-cost bond fund will cost .8% or less. A low-cost American stock fund will cost less than 1%, while a low-cost foreign stock fund should cost less than 1.25%. You should seek to invest with funds that have similar, or even lower, annual expenses.

This is not to say that a fund with higher annual expenses might not be a good fund over the next 10 years. It may very well turn out to be a big winner. Or it may be a below average fund. Paying higher expenses will not guarantee that your fund is going to be better than average, but high expenses does mean that your fund must earn just that much more money before the shareholders earn anything. Studies that have measured annual expenses and the return on mutual funds have concluded that high expenses are a drag on performance. All things being equal, you are better off with lower expenses.

The average variable annuity charges around 2% a year for annual expenses. As a result, you should expect variable annuity performance, on average, to trail the results of the lower cost mutual funds. This is not to say that some variable annuity funds might not outperform most mutual funds. It will happen. But most variable annuities fund's performance will be dragged down by the high expenses.

There are some variable annuities that do have lower annual expenses. These are the "no-load" variable annuities. Many of these represent a partnership between a life insurance company and a no-load mutual fund company. These variable annuities may have annual expenses of around 1% a year, and no surrender charges.

The last area to consider when evaluating mutual funds is the performance track record. However, the past investment performance of a mutual fund is not as important as you might think. Many investors think that if you pick a mutual fund that has had good investment performance in the past, that will guarantee that it will have good performance in the future. However, studies conducted in this area indicate that there is little or no predictive value to a mutual fund's past performance.

As an example, if there are 100 mutual funds that specialize in large, American corporation stocks, you will be able to identify the 10 who had the best performance over the last 5 years. You might think that if you bought one of those funds, you would be more likely to have much better than average performance over the next 5 years. Studies have shown that is not true. Some of those funds may do better than average over the next 5 years, but some will do worse. There does not appear to be any real predictive value to past performance. This may run contrary to what you are told by stockbrokers and financial magazines, but all the studies confirm it. However, studies have shown that funds which have poor past performance are more likely to continue to have poor performance in the future. It is thought that part of the reason why that is true has to do with many poor performing funds having higher than usual annual expenses which always remain as a drag on performance.

All of this creates a dilemma for the investor. How should you try to pick your funds if past performance is such a rotten guide for the future? It would seem that there must be some method that is better than just throwing a dart at the mutual fund section of the paper and buying the mutual fund which you hit (although some studies indicate that the dart method will work as well as relying on the average stockbroker's choice). Here are two suggestions.

In the first, you would obtain a listing of mutual funds sorted by investment style. The list should give you the 5-year performance of the fund, its annual expenses, and whether it is a load or no-load fund. You can obtain this information from a number of sources. FORBES MAGAZINE puts out a very good annual review of mutual funds every Fall in one of its issues. Other magazines such as FORTUNE, BARRONS and MONEY also put out such listings. The WALL STREET JOURNAL also publishes a complete listing of mutual fund performance and expenses every quarter. Your local newspaper may as well. Some of these listings may even "rate" the mutual funds based on a number of factors including past performance, although you will have to decide for yourself if the ratings really have any value if past performance is such a rotten guide of future performance.

From one of these listings, you should pick a mutual fund whose investment goals and restrictions match yours, which has below average annual expenses, which is a no-load, and whose past performance is in the top 25% of all funds of the same category. If, after receiving and reading a copy of its prospectus, it seems to met your needs, you can go ahead and use that fund. This method of selecting a fund should work as well as any other method. You may take this one step further and buy a fund that was in the top 10%, or even #1, but it is unlikely that you will really improve your odds of getting a better than average fund that way. In any event, you will end up with a low cost, no-load fund with a good track record. Your typical stockbroker is not going to do any better.

The second method is even easier. After you have decided on what type of mutual fund you want to own, go out a invest in a low-cost, no-load, index fund of that type. For example, if you want to put money into a large American corporation stock fund (a "blue chip" stock fund), you would buy a S&P500 Index fund. You know that this fund will never be #1, but you also know it will predictably beat the majority of actively managed blue chip stock funds.

Many investors are convinced that there must be some secret "system" that would allow them to pick a better-than-average mutual fund. However, all of the studies conducted indicate that such a system does not appear to exist. In fact, as you will learn later in the book, the choice of mutual fund or fund manager is not even the most important part of the decision making process.

CHAPTER EIGHT

CALCULATING YOUR CONTRIBUTIONS

One of the great advantages that 403(b) plans have over 401(k)s is the ability to defer a greater part of your income. However, this benefit comes at the expense of making the process a bit complicated. In this chapter, we will try to give a simple explanation of your options. The key areas include:

* **THE BASIC CONTRIBUTION RULES**

* **SPECIAL RULES FOR PEOPLE ABOUT TO RETIRE**

* **SPECIAL RULES FOR PEOPLE WHO WANT TO "CATCH UP" FOR PAST YEARS**

* **SPECIAL RULES FOR CHURCH EMPLOYEES**

Although the forms you get from your employer or investment provider look daunting, it is not really that hard to figure it all out. You just need to take it step by step.

THE GENERAL CONTRIBUTION RULES

One important area in which 403(b) plans have an advantage over other plans, such as 401(k)s, is in the amount you are annually allowed to defer and invest into these plans.

With a 401(k) plan, your annual contributions are limited to the lesser of 15% of your compensation, or $9,240. If your employer also contributes to your 401(k), or to another defined contribution plan such as a profit sharing plan, the total of your contributions and their contributions cannot exceed 25% of your gross compensation, or $30,000 (this is known in the IRS Code as the "Section 415" limit).

By comparison, the rules for 403(b)s allow you to defer a greater amount under the general rules. There are a number of special provisions that allow the basic 403(b) levels to be exceeded. For many employees, particularly those who are younger and not as established financially, the higher levels may not have any real importance. They can be hard-pressed to contribute even 5% or 10%. However, the higher maximum contribution levels and special provisions can allow employees to "catch up" when they are older and financially better off, something that 401(k) plans do not permit.

BASIC RULES AND DEFINITIONS

A few basic rules that you should be aware of before you start calculating your maximum deduction (or "salary reduction" as the IRS views it).

For starters, you may make a new salary reduction agreement with your employer only once per tax year. That is, if you ask your employer to withhold a certain dollar amount or percentage this tax year, you must wait until a future tax year to change that amount. You may drop the salary reduction entirely at any point, but you may not otherwise change the amount or percentage a second time during the current tax year. The tax year is your individual tax year, which for almost all taxpayers is the calendar year. If you change which life insurance company or mutual fund receives your contributions that will NOT count as a new salary reduction agreement. In addition, if you agree to a percentage salary reduction and during the year you receive a raise, the fact that the percentage reduction will now apply to a larger salary will not count as a new agreement.

If you contribute more money into your 403(b) than the maximum contribution rules permit, you will have to pay taxes on the excess contribution in the year the money is contributed. The excess contribution will appear on your W-2 form as earned income. You will also have to pay taxes on it a second time in the year that the money is withdrawn. Paying taxes twice on the same money is not a good idea and you will want to avoid over-contributions. There is one exception to paying taxes twice on the over-contribution. If you over contribute in one year, and withdraw the over-contribution before April 15th of the following year, you will not be taxed twice.

It sometimes happens that employers also contribute to your 403(b). This is uncommon, but it is possible. If they contribute on a "matching" basis where they put money in only if you put money in, by all means take them up on the offer. It is a great deal. However, it is more common that the employer, if making contributions to a retirement plan on your behalf, will be contributing to a different plan than your 403(b). For example, to a pension plan.

The compensation that you use in the calculations is the compensation from your 403(b) eligible employer only. If you also work for another employer, you may not combine the two sets of income. There is an exception for church employees who work for related church employers.

The examples given assume that you are a full-time employee working for a full year. If you are not a full-time employee, you must treat each year in which you were a part-time employee as a partial year when adding up your years of service with an employer. For example, if you have worked half-time for the last 8 years, you have 4 years of service for the purposes of the maximum contribution calculations. Similarly, when calculating your annual compensation for the purposes of figuring the "exclusion allowance" below, you would use the total of this year and last year's gross compensation to arrive at a full-year, full-time salary.

You do not have to work 40 hours a week, or 12 months a year, to be a full-time employee under the 403(b) rules. The determination is based on what is customary for your position. A professor who teaches 16 hours a week, or a teacher who works 9 months out of the year, would both be considered full-time employees if that amount of work was customary for full-time employees performing the same service.

If your annuity contract contains any sort of incidental life insurance benefit above and beyond your retirement annuity benefit, the portion of your payments that pay for that incidental life insurance benefit remains taxable.

The IRS has a somewhat quirky way of viewing gross compensation. Most employees view the amount going into their 403(b) as a deduction from their gross salary. The IRS views it as a reduction in your salary, in exchange for having the employer contribute the funds to your 403(b) account. The result is that what you think of as gross income or compensation, and what the IRS thinks of gross compensation, are not the same. If you will be paid $40,000 this year, and agree to have $4,000 put into a 403(b) account, you still tend to think of your gross salary as $40,000. To the IRS, your gross compensation is $36,000.

Finally, the IRS calculates whether or not you exceed your maximum contribution level after the fact. Many of their worksheets and examples assume that you already put money into the 403(b) account during the year, the year is over, and now you are calculating whether you put too much in or not. But individuals tend to view the process looking forward, and are trying to determine ahead of time how much they can put in without exceeding their tax-deductible limits. The result is that the IRS calculations may appear somewhat odd and stilted to most employees.

MAXIMUM CONTRIBUTION RULES

Under the general rules governing 403(b), your maximum contribution limit is the **LESSER** of the following three figures.

One:
An annual limit of $9,500. If the employee is also covered by a second salary reduction plan, such as a 401(k) or SEP-IRA, the combination of the two cannot exceed $9,500. In future years, this fixed dollar limit will increase with inflation.

Two:
An amount equal to the employee's "exclusion allowance". This figure represents prior year contribution activity. You calculate this amount by multiplying your most recent year's compensation by 20%, multiple that number by the number of years of service you have with your employer, and subtract the total of all the amounts previously contributed to retirement plans by you AND your employer, including 403(b)s, 401(k)s, and pension plans (if your employer does not tell you how much they contribute on your behalf, IRS Publication 571 has a formula for estimating the amount). What is left over will be how much "unused" contributions you are deemed to have left for future use. When you make this calculation, you count the current year as one full year. You also use as your compensation your salary AFTER you have subtracted your current year contribution. For example, if your gross salary is $40,000 before you

have a deduction of $4,000 for your 403(b), than the calculation is done using the $36,000 figure.

Three: *You and your employer may not contribute to all of your defined contribution plans an amount greater than 25% of your compensation, or $30,000. So if you are covered by a 403(b) and another defined contribution plan, or if your employer contributes to your 403(b), the total of the two sets of contributions may not exceed this limit. This is the IRS Section 415 limit.*

These calculations are per employee, not per household. So if both you and your spouse are eligible to use 403(b)s, the calculations are based on your individual compensation and years of service.

If you look at the three calculations, you will see that you may generally contribute up to 25% into your 403(b) annually, up to $9,500; but because of the exclusion allowance, in the long run you may only average 20% per year. If you wish to maximize your contributions, you must work out the three figures from above and select the lowest number. The official IRS tables for calculating these figures are found in Appendix A, Worksheet 1 and 2. You may also wish to get a copy of IRS Publication 571, which contains further information about contribution limits.

If you intend to contribute an amount below the basic maximum figures, you may not need to spend much time going through the tables.

EXAMPLE:
If you plan to contribute 10%, and you have a pre-contribution salary of $40,000, you are not likely to bump into a maximum contribution limit. Your contribution, in dollars, is only $4,000, well below the $9,500 limit. Your percentage limit is also far below both the section 415 limit of 25%, and the exclusion amount. Remember that the exclusion limit calculation counts 20% of the current year after-deduction salary of $36,000, so even if you have maxed out your contributions in past years, you have 20% for this year.

If you have never contributed to your 403(b) in the past, and you have a number of years of service, you may find that your "unused" exclusion allowance figure is a large number.

EXAMPLE:
You have work at a school district for 12 years, and have never contributed to a 403(b) in the past. Your salary, before the 403(b) deduction, is $44,000. To keep the example simple, we will assume that

your employer contributes nothing to any other type of retirement plan. You will earn $40,000 after your employer withholds $4,000 for a 403(b) this year. Your exclusion allowance is 20% x $40,000 x 12 YEARS - zero past contributions = $96,000. It will be a long time before the exclusion allowance figure will impact your current maximum contribution.

If you wish to contribute an amount near the limits above, you will need to go through the charts and calculate your exact limit.

However, you may wish to contribute MORE than the basic contribution limits allow.

SPECIAL CONTRIBUTION CALCULATION RULES

For example, you may be 55 years of age and intending to retire at age 62. In the past, you may not have contributed the maximum each year because you were busy buying a home and raising a family. You are now in the position to save more, and you want to invest as much as you can over the next few years.

There are a number of alternative methods of calculating maximum contributions. Each method raises one or more of the three limits already discussed, under certain circumstances. These special rules apply only if your employer is an educational organization, hospital, home health service agency, church or church-related organization. So not all 403(b) eligible employees can use these methods.

The IRS charts for these methods are found in Appendix A, but we will give a summary of each method below.

One special method of calculating your maximum is available to someone in their last year of service with an employer. This method is known under IRS regulations as the **"Year of Separation from Service Limit"**.

Under this method, you can drop the 25% annual limit under Section 415. You may also forget about the $9,500 annual limit. You will calculate a special exclusion allowance which is based on the last 10 years of service ONLY. You can contribute a maximum of the lesser of this special modified 10-year exclusion allowance, or $30,000. This could permit you to make one large final contribution before you separate from your employer.

EXAMPLE:

You are the principal of a school who will retire this year. Your annual salary is $50,000. You have contributed only $12,000 to your 403(b) over the last 10 years. The school district contributed $20,000 over the last ten years to a teachers pension plan on your behalf. Your special exclusion is 20% times $50,000 times 10 years minus prior total contributions. That is .20 x $50,000 x 10 - $20,000 = $80,000. In this example, your special maximum exclusion figure is more than the $30,000 limit. So you can contribute $30,000 in your last year.

The IRS chart for this option is "Worksheet 3" in Appendix A. You may make use of this special calculation only ONCE in your lifetime.

The next method is called the **"ANY YEAR LIMIT"**. In this method, you substitute for the 25% limit of Sec. 415 the lesser of the following three figures:

One:
   $4,000 plus 25% of your compensation for the current year.

Two:
   Your exclusion allowance.

Three:
   $15,000.

EXAMPLE:
   You earn $29,000 and have been with a hospital for 17 years. During that time, you contributed a total of $14,400 to a 403(b), and the hospital contributed $20,000 to a pension plan. You want to contribute $9,000 this year to the 403(b), so that you will receive $20,000 of salary this year.

Calculation One) $4,000 + .25 of $20,000 = $9,000

Calculation Two-Exclusion Limit) .20 x $20,000 x 17 - $34,400 = $33,600

Calculation Three) $15,000

Based on the three calculations above, the lowest figure is $9,000. You may contribute a maximum of $9,000. Please see "Worksheet 4" in Appendix A.

Another method is called the *"OVERALL LIMIT"*.

In this calculation, you drop the use of the exclusion allowance. Instead you use the sec. 415 limits of 25% or $30,000.

Example:
You are employed by a college and earn $25,000 a year. Your limit is the lesser of $30,000, or 25% x $25,000 = $6,250.

Please refer to "Worksheet 5" in Appendix A.

You may only make use of one of the above special methods of calculating. For example, if you elect in one year to use the Overall Limit, you may not in future years use the Any Year Limit or the Year of Separation from Service Limit. You must continue use the Overall Limit or the basic calculation limits.

SPECIAL RULES FOR LONG-TIME EMPLOYEES

A method exists for employees who have been with their employers for 15 or more years. This is also a special catch-up provision. In this case, the $9,500 annual limit under the basic contribution rules is increased by the **LESSER** of the three following figures.

One:
$3,000. This would make your annual limit $12,500.

Two:
$15,000 minus prior year contributions in excess of the $9,500 made under this catch-up rule. So if you use this catch-up provision, you may only use it until you have contributed an extra $15,000.

Three:
$5,000 times the number of years of service minus the total elective deferrals made in earlier years.

Please see "Worksheet 6" in Appendix A.

SPECIAL RULES FOR CHURCH EMPLOYEES

Finally, there is a special rule that only applies to employees of churches or related church groups. Under this method, there are a few changes.

First, if you have worked for a number of different employers within your church over your career, you will count them as one employer.

Second, if your annual adjusted gross income, excluding earnings of your spouse, is $17,000 a year or less, you have a minimum exclusion contribution amount of $3,000 (or your earnings for the year, if they are less than $3,000), even if the general rule would give you a lesser figure.

Finally, you may elect to have up to $10,000 contributed a year, even if this exceeds the section 415 25% rule. However, your lifetime total extra contributions under this special rule may not exceed $40,000.

At this point, you may need a bit of a breather. All of the above options tend to confuse employees as to which one to apply. If you are not planning on maximizing your contributions, you don't need to worry about any of them. However, if you do wish to defer as much as possible, you will need to run all of the methods which may apply to you to determine which one will permit you the maximum contribution. So, unless you are a church employee who has worked more than 15 years for the church, not contributed a lot in the past, and you are in your last year of service, it is unlikely that you will have to run all of the computations.

CHAPTER NINE

RETIREMENT PLANNING

This is the chapter in which we bring together the decision-making process. The key questions to answer before you start to fill in the forms. Most of financial planning is common sense.

*   **WHAT IS FINANCIAL PLANNING?**

*   **HOW MUCH SHOULD I CONTRIBUTE?**

*   **THE IMPORTANCE OF ASSET ALLOCATION**

*   **RISK VERSUS REWARD**

*   **HOW VARIOUS ASSET TYPES WORK**

*   **INFLATION: THE LURKING THREAT**

*   **YOUR LIFESTYLE AND YOUR CHOICES**

*   **RULES TO LIVE BY**

Even the best tool is useless in the hands of someone who does not know how to use it. Financial planning is the ability to use the tools. It is not difficult, but it does require you to stop and think.

WHAT IS FINANCIAL PLANNING?

Entire books have been written on the subject of financial planning for the individual. It would not be possible to do more than touch the surface in a single chapter. This chapter will focus on financial planning as it applies to your 403(b) retirement account. There are several key ideas that all 403(b) investors need to understand about investing.

The process of bringing together all the facts and decisions concerning your retirement planning is part of a process called "financial planning". Although many investment professionals will attempt to convince you that it is a process that should not be attempted without professional guidance (usually theirs), the fact is that it is mostly about making logical, common-sense decisions. Any reasonably intelligent person can handle his or her own financial plans. Most investment professionals that you encounter are professional salesmen more then anything else. Most of them, despite their fancy titles, don't really know much more about real financial planning then the average investor. Don't let their doomsaying stop you from taking control of your own finances.

When you boil it all down, there are TWO questions you must answer concerning your 403(b) when deciding on your course of action. The first is how much should you try to defer in your 403(b) each year? The second is once you have deferred the money from your salary into your plan, how should you split the money up among your various choices?

HOW MUCH SHOULD I CONTRIBUTE?

Many people get stuck at this first question, unsure of how to decide. In fact, like many major questions, it is a matter of using the process of elimination. The guiding principle to remember is that the more money you defer and invest now, the more money you will have in the future. The less money you defer now, the less money you will have in the future.

It is possible to calculate all sorts of possible outcomes using a calculator or computer program, and match them against some possible future income needs. But even the fanciest computer program is merely doing fairly simple future value calculations, given certain inputs about contribution levels, starting balances, rates of return, inflation, salary growth and time until retirement.

NOTE: All investors are advised to obtain a hand held-calculator that can run such future value calculations [the author uses a Texas Instrument BA-35]. Most have pre-designated keys which allow you to quickly calculate the answers to future value calculations. For example, if you enter your current 403(b) account balance, your monthly contribution level, your time until retirement, and your estimated long-term return from your investment, the calculator will tell you what would be your ending 403(b) balance (future value). You may also use the same process to do calculations regarding other areas of your finances including, for example, your home mortgage.

Remember, all of these numbers are merely projections based on your estimates. The results you get are merely an indication of where you might stand 20 years from now at retirement. Your actual results cannot be known ahead of time. The basic premise when deciding on how much to save in your 403(b) is as simple as whether you want more, or less, money in your future.

A key factor in deciding how much to defer is to consider what other resources you have, or expect to have, at retirement aside from your 403(b). If you anticipate having a large amount of resources because of other investments, a pension, social security, an inheritance, etc., then your future 403(b) balance will not be a critical factor in your future financial situation. However, most people are not going to find themselves independently wealthy at retirement. For them, the assets in their 403(b)s may represent a large portion of their retirement assets. The answer to the question of "how much should I save" is "as much as you possible can" (although this may seem an overly simple answer to what should be a complicated question, perhaps you should ask yourself the flip side of the question, "is it possible to save too much"?.)

As was mentioned earlier, the actual decision can be approached using the process of elimination. We know you cannot defer less than 0%. We also know that for most people, you cannot defer on a long term basis more than 20% of your salary, or $9,500, per year (the exceptions to these limits were discussed in the previous chapter). So your answer must fall usually somewhere between 0% and 20%.

We can narrow this range down even further. If you are serious about saving for the future, you will probably need to try to save at least 4%-5% as a minimum. On the other end, many people would be hard pressed to maintain an acceptable life style if they reduced their current income by 20%. For those people, the highest acceptable contribution might be 10%-15%. Of course, there are those employees who have enough household income because of a working spouse or other income that they will try to go for the maximum contribution possible, particularly if the other working spouse is NOT covered by any sort of retirement plan.

86

For most employees, the answer will lay somewhere between 5% and 15%. Remember the guiding principle, the more you save now, the more you will have later. You should try to save as much as you can. For most people, this means trying to save an amount closer to 10%-15%. It may sound hard. That's because it is hard to forgo current spending and enjoyment for future spending, but that is the essence of saving for the future. You may take your calculator and use it to project how much you will have at retirement using the percentage that you elect to use. If you prefer, you can use a computer program to run all sorts of charts and projections and print them in color. The rock bottom answer for most people will be the same. You need to save as much as you can.

One of the advantages of 403(b)s over other plans is that they do allow you to bump up your maximum contribution limits in your later years in some cases. Younger workers, who tend to under contribute because of competing financial needs, can use some of these methods to catch up in their later working years when they are more financially established. Of course, in the unlikely event you actually save TOO much money for the future, you can always cut back contributions, retire early, or spend more lavishly.

Once you have decided on how much to add on a yearly basis, you will need to decide on where to put your future contributions, as well as any money you have already accumulated. This brings up the heart of financial planning, Asset Allocation.

THE IMPORTANCE OF ASSET ALLOCATION

Asset Allocation, in its simplest form, is nothing more than deciding how you will invest your money given several distinctly different investment options. For example, if you had a choice of investing your money between a fixed annuity, a money market fund, a U.S. Government bond fund, and a blue chip stock fund, the percentage you put into each category is your asset allocation. Asset Allocation is about choosing between TYPES or STYLES of investments. It is not about choosing, within a given type of investment, WHO will handle your money. This is an important distinction.

Many studies have been performed over the last fifty years to try to identify what are the key factors in investing. Many of these studies have focused on the investing habits of retirement plans. What has been discovered is that the most important decisions affecting the eventual results for the retirement plan is how the money was invested in the various categories, not who managed the money within each category. In fact, several studies have indicated that well over 90% of the final results depend on the allocations chosen.

Let me give you an example of how this might affect an individual. You are given an investment choice for your 403(b) that consists of three different life insurance companies or mutual fund families. Each of the three firms offers you the same four investment options. Those options are a money market fund, a fixed annuity with an interest rate set annually, a U.S. Government bond fund, and a blue chip stock fund. You must invest your money with one of the companies, and you can split up your money in any fashion among the investment options. The studies show that decision you make about how to split up your money will be responsible for over 90% of the long-term outcome. The company you hire will effect less than 10% of the results.

The point to be learned here is the importance of the decision you make about the categories of investments you make, as opposed to the firm you use to handle those categories. It is not uncommon to see people spend hours and hours trying to decide between two different mutual fund families or insurance companies. They may then spend only a few minutes picking out which types of funds to actually use for their investments. This is wrong. The primary decision should be the type of investment. This is also why you were told in earlier chapters that all your employer really needs to give you is a fairly small number of options to choose from, as long as these choices were of different investment types. A selection list that gives you 50 different varieties of the same type of investment is not really an advantage to you, particularly if you have to pay a lot to use any of them.

RISK VERSUS REWARD

Nowhere in the world does the notion that there is no free lunch show up more clearly than in investing. All investments present you with some balance between the risks you assume, and the rewards you seek. If you want to have low risk, you can't plan on high returns. If you seek higher returns, you must accept higher risks. Reward is a concept that is easy to understand. We measure it by what return, usually expressed as a percentage on an annual basis, that an investment has returned in the past, or is expected to return in the future. By contrast, Risk is a more complicated concept.

Some people think of Risk in terms of just losing money. In fact, Risk is more than that. Risk is not only the possibility of negative returns (losing money). It is also the concept of uncertainty. For example, let us say you have two investments. One will always return 10% every year. The other will average 10% a year, but its actual year by year results will fluctuate between 5% and 15%. Neither investment will ever lose money. Even though neither investment will ever lose money, and both average 10% a year, financial analysts would say that the second investment is riskier because it is less certain year by year.

Financial analysts generally say that Risks comes in several distinct varieties. One is Credit or Default Risk. This is the risk that a financial promise made to you will not meet. For example, the risk that an insurance company that issued you a fixed annuity becomes insolvent and cannot meet the terms of the annuity. Or the risk that some of the corporations that issued bonds purchased by your corporate bond mutual fund fail to make interest or principal payments.

Another type of Risk is Market Risk. This is the risk that the market or resale value of an investment that you own will rise or fall. For example, the rise or fall in the market price of stocks or bonds. Even U.S. Government bonds, which are assumed to have little or no Credit Risk, are effected by Market Risk. You will remember that the market value of bonds changes between when the bond was issued and when it will mature. This change is caused by changes in the prevailing rates of interest.

Another type of Risk is Liquidity Risk. This represents the risk faced in investments that cannot be readily turned into cash. A good example of investments that are faced with this type of risk is real estate.

Finally there is the Risk created by Inflation. This is also called Purchasing Power Risk. This is the risk that your investment will not grow and keep pace with inflation. By conventional measure, an investor who owned an investment in 1960 which was worth $10,000, and which is worth $20,000 today, has not lost anything. However, taking inflation into account, that investor has been dealt a heavy blow. Many investors will say that they will not take ANY Risk, and will put all of their money in bank accounts, money markets or T-Bills. These investors find out the much more subtle effect of Inflation Risk.

NO INVESTMENT AVOIDS ALL FORMS OF RISK. It is not a practical plan to say that you want a "risk-free" investment. They do not exist. Each type of investment displays some form of risks to go with the returns you might expect. What you must do is evaluate your situation and decide on which forms of Risk you are willing to live with in your investment portfolio.

When deciding on an investment portfolio, professional portfolio managers will usually take a look at five factors in trying to decide about Risks and Returns. Those factors are:

1) Time Horizon of the portfolio,
2) Cash or Liquidity needs of the portfolio,
3) Legal or other constraints on the investment choices,
4) Tax consequences of the portfolio,
5) Any other special circumstances.

Let us apply these factors to 403(b) portfolio.

Time Horizon

Unlike some investment portfolios, you usually have a good idea of how long your money will remain invested. It is earmarked for a set purpose, retirement. You usually can estimate how long it is before you will actually use the money. Maybe you will start to use the money when you are 55, maybe when you are 65 or 70. Armed with that information, you can make some judgments about your expected time horizon and the various types of risk which may effect you. If you have 20 years until you are going to use the money, you can afford to live with Market Risk. After all, you have time to wait out the market. However, you should be concerned about Inflation Risk. Over 20 years, inflation can do a great deal of damage to a "low risk", low return investment. If you are retiring next year, the opposite scenario would be true. One year of inflation is unlikely to hurt you. But you do not have time to necessarily ride out a down market.

Liquidity Needs

Because this is a retirement account, unless you are already retired you may have little or no need for your investments to be easily accessible or be able to be turned into cash in a short amount of time. You would not need to invest heavily in liquid investments such as money markets, or worry about how much cash income your investments currently produce. However, for those who are retired and planning on living off their 403(b), the reverse may be true.

Legal, Tax & Special Constraints

Legal and Tax constraints are very simple for 403(b)s. You already know that you are limited to annuities and mutual funds as investment options. Your range of choices may be further limited by your employer. You also already know that you will not pay any taxes on money while it is inside the plan.

Finally, Special Circumstances is exactly that, something unique to your situation that will affect what you do. For example, if you have an adult child who will always need financial support, even after you have died, this may affect the strategy you employ. However, most people do not have unique circumstances which will impact their 403(b).

For the majority of 403(b) investors, the one factor that they will most use in deciding on their investment portfolio is the first one factor, the TIME HORIZON.

ASSET CATEGORIES

Chapter 6 and 7 have already given you a pretty clear idea of what your choices are with 403(b)s. For the purposes of asset allocation, you can break down your options into a small number of categories. Those major categories are:

Fixed annuity-annual interest rate,
Fixed annuity-multiple year interest rate,
Money Market Funds,
Bond Funds
  High Quality Bonds   &   Short-Term
  Low Quality Bonds   Medium-Term
  Foreign Bonds   Long-Term
Stock Funds
  Large American Stocks
  Small American Stocks
  Foreign Stocks
  Specialty Funds.

When it comes time for you to pick your investments, you will be mostly selecting from the above asset categories. Let us review each category from a Risk and Return standpoint, paying particular attention to how the asset category behaves over time.

Fixed Annuities are not subject to Market Risk. The insurance company prevents that. However, since you are dependent on the life insurance company's promise, your are faced with Default Risk. Liquidity is usually a problem only to the extent of paying sales charges to get out, or facing tax penalties for using the money early. There is a certain amount of uncertainty depending on whether you have an interest rate that resets every year, or every few years. Over the long-term, if you pick your annuity carefully, you should be able to earn a little more than inflation. But you must remember that the life insurance company has no desire to pay you any more for the use of your money than they must to keep your deposit. It is very unlikely that over a period of years a fixed annuity will produce spectacular results.

You should remember that most life insurance companies invest your money into bonds, usually bonds with high credit ratings. Since how much the life insurance company earns on these bonds is a major factor in determining how much they will pay you (minus the company's overhead), you should not be surprised to find out that, in the long run, your return on the fixed annuity will tend to mimic the returns on bonds, minus the life insurance company's overhead.

Money Market funds lack any meaningful Default Risk or Market Risk. They also tend to be very liquid. However, in the long run, they are very much at risk to Inflation. By definition, they cannot earn more than the returns on the short-term, high-quality debt investments, such as Treasury Bills, that they purchase for the fund's portfolio. Over the years, the returns on money market investments have varied, but they do not offer you a realistic chance to gain on inflation over the long haul. Money market funds are useful in 403(b) plans mostly as a temporary "parking place" for your money, someplace to keep the money when it is not in another type of investment.

Bond funds come in a number of varieties. Most investors steer away from funds that buy low rated bonds, or foreign bonds. After all, if you are willing to take the greater risk of those types of funds, you might as well invest into a stock fund where the potential returns would be greater too.

A high-rated bond fund, perhaps a U.S. Government bond-only fund, would have little or no Default Risk. How much Market Risk you experience is mostly a matter of how long term are the bonds in the portfolio. A fund with mostly short-term bonds (1-5 year maturities) would experience very little market fluctuation. A medium-term bond fund (5-10 year) would earn more interest, but also fluctuate more. Long-term bond funds (10+ years) tend to earn the most interest and fluctuate the most.

Although bonds may show strong market fluctuation in a given year, over the long-term the ups and downs tend to cancel out. This is because the market value of the bonds will change from day-to-day or month-to-month, but the ultimate maturity value of the bonds remains the same. The market price of a bond will be drawn towards its maturity value. Furthermore, the actual amount of interest that the fund collects from a bonds is usually constant. When viewed over longer-term horizons, high quality bond funds can show surprising consistency. For example, a long-term U.S. Government bond fund might start off with a share price of $10 per share. It might be earning around 8% from the bonds, or approximately $0.80 per year in interest from the bonds per share. Over a ten-year period of time, the price may fluctuate between $9 and $11 as prevailing interest rates jump around, but at the end of ten years it might still be in the area of $10. But every year the $.80 of interest is earned. You really make your money in bonds off the interest that rolls in year after year. If you reinvest your interest into the bond fund, it will be the power of compounding interest that drives up your account value. However, bonds, like fixed annuities, have historically done only a little better than inflation.

Many financial analysts would hold that for a long-term investor, there is not much difference between buying a fixed annuity and a medium-term, high quality bond fund in terms of the risk over time and the investment returns that they may receive.

Stock Funds are not affected much by Default Risks, but they are clearly affected by Market Risks. Stock prices can jump around a lot, particularly in the short-term. Large American corporation stocks ("blue chips"), as a group, have tended since World War II to show gains in three out of four years. That means that you can expect losses one fourth of the time if you buy and hold stocks for one year. Since you are investing for retirement, you may have a longer anticipated holding period. For investors that buy and hold their stocks for five years, the odds tilt even more in their favor. Since World War II, investors who invested in the stock market for a five-year period of time would have made money about 19 times out of 20. In fact, there has only been one really bad five-year period of time for owning stocks since the war. During the early 70's, there actually were two back-to-back down years. It is clear that, at least in the past, the risk of actually losing money by investing into American stocks on a diversified basis is fairly low if you are a long-term investor.

As a trade off to their market price volatility, stocks have traditionally done very well on the return side. Since World War II, blue chip stocks have returned an average of around 11%-12% per year. But that average may make it seem smoother than it really is in the real world. In fact, blue chip stocks tend to produce annual returns that may AVERAGE 11%-12%, but the actual year by year returns tend to fall within a range of -10% to +30%. So stocks make a good long-term investment, but you still have a fair measure of ups and downs to live with along the way. The returns on stocks over the years have tended to greatly outperform inflation (after all, as inflation causes prices to rise over time, corporations simply raise their prices, and ultimately their profits). For an investor looking ten to twenty years down the road, stocks seem to be a logical candidate for their portfolio.

Smaller American stocks and foreign stocks tend to have even greater return potential than large American stocks, but the year-by-year fluctuations are also greater. You may wish to select them as an investment option if you have a great deal of time until you will use your investment funds, or if you are comfortable with accepting the greater year-to-year fluctuation in order to try and earn a greater return.

Most Specialty Funds tend to be more narrowly focused or extreme versions of one of the other categories. For example, an American stock fund that only buys computer company stocks. Because they tend to "put all of their eggs in one basket", most specialty funds have higher risk and return profiles compared to a more conventional, broadly diversified fund. As a general rule, only a fairly knowledgeable investor should look at most Specialty Funds.

One exception with Specialty Funds concerning risk is those types of mutual funds called Index Funds. Index Funds tend to be very broadly diversified, frequently owning all of the stocks found in a particular Index which measures some part of the investment market. As a result, the risk level of a Index Fund tends to be the same as the average risk level of the entire market.

Balanced Funds and Asset Allocation Funds are generally a mixture of stocks and bonds. As a result, they tend to have fluctuation levels and investment returns that fall between the results of a bond fund and a stock fund.

If you wanted to neatly classify all of the categories, you could say that most fixed annuities, money market funds, and high quality, short and medium-term bond funds represent the lower risk, lower return options. Long-term, high-quality bond funds and blue chip stock funds, including most index funds, represent the middle range of risk and return. The rest of the choices tend to represent the higher risk, higher return options.

DIVERSIFICATION

An integral concept that is part of Asset Allocation and Financial Planning is the notion of Diversification. Diversification involves spreading your investments out to avoid the risk that a bad result in one area will affect your entire portfolio. Diversification can be found within the asset type you select. For example, a blue chip stock fund might take your money and invest it in the stocks of 100 companies, spread out over 15 different industries. If something bad happens to one company, or even an entire industry, it will have cause only a limited amount of damage to the entire portfolio. Or you might make use of 2 or 3 different life insurance companies over time to handle your fixed annuities, figuring that if one company runs into trouble, you don't have all your fixed annuity assets tied up with them.

Diversification is also part of the asset allocation process. And there is a special twist to it. You know that different types of investments have different Risk/Reward relationships. When you buy a stock fund, you generally expect a higher Reward, and a higher Risk, than a U.S. Government bond fund. If you could quantify the Risk and Reward of both of the investment categories, you might come up with a scale that says that the Risk of a 100% stock fund is a "20", and its expected Reward is "12"; while the Risk of a bond fund is a "10", and the expected Reward is a "6" (the numbers themselves are completely arbitrary and merely serve to make an illustration). If you own the bonds and you want to increase your potential Reward by investing in stocks, you will increase your expected Risk. The saying "there is no such thing as a free lunch" seems to apply here.

If you mix the two types of investments together, say 50/50, you would expect an overall average Reward on the mixed portfolio that is less than owning stocks, but more than owning bonds, and an overall Risk that is less than stocks, but more than bonds. In fact, you might expect the new, mixed portfolio to have a Risk and expected Reward that is exactly midway between the two, which would be a Risk of "15" and an expected Reward "9". Seems simple and logical. That is not what happens.

What financial observers have actually noted is that the Risk in the mixed portfolio drops faster than the change in expected Reward on the mixed portfolio. You might still end up with a expected Reward of 9%, as predicted, but the Risk might be only 13, not the 15 you expected. In other words, the Risk/Reward relationship of the mixed portfolio is actually better than the Risk/Reward relationship of either of the two parts of the mixed portfolio.

There are some lengthy mathematical reasons why this phenomenon occurs, and it would take an entire book to cover the subject. The economist who did much of the work in this area, Harry Markowitz, actually won the Nobel Prize for Economics for his analysis. However, the key concept is that the average annual amount of fluctuations of the stock and bond portfolios, which many economists use as a mathematical representation of the portfolio's overall risk, tend to partially cancel each other out.

The following is a very simple example of how this works:

Let us assume that the stock portfolio every year is always either up 20%, or down 20%. We also assume that the bond portfolio is always either up 10%, or down 10%.

If the two portfolios always fluctuated together, your mixed portfolio would be always either be up 15%, or down 15%, every year. This is what you may have expected.

However, what if the stocks and bonds NEVER fluctuate together? Stocks are always up 20% while the bonds are down 10%, so the mixed portfolio is up 10%; or bonds are up 10% while stocks are down 20%, and the mixed portfolio is down 10%. The mixed portfolio would always be either up or down only 10%.

Now, what if stocks and bonds sometimes fluctuate together, and sometimes they don't (this is actually what happens). In that case, depending on how much their fluctuations coincide, the mixed portfolio will fluctuate somewhere between 10% and 15%.

Despite the reduction in annual fluctuation, the annual average return of the mixed portfolio over 10-years is still going to remain 9%.

A word of caution. The reduction in fluctuation occurs if two different investments fluctuate separately from each other. If they tend to fluctuate together, the effect is reduced or eliminated. For example, if you invest in two different blue chip American stock funds, they will tend to fluctuate together. You may get little or no reduction in fluctuation by mixing the two into a portfolio. Real diversification means investing in different types of investments, not buying different versions of the same thing. You don't really accomplish much in the way of diversification by investing in 5 different mutual funds that all invest in essentially the same thing, whether its bonds or blue chip stocks. But if one of the funds buys blue chip stocks, one buys bonds, one buys foreign stocks, one buys small American stocks, and one is a money market, then you have real diversification.

The important thing to bear in mind is that this power of diversification is a valuable advantage. It can allow you to invest in a mixture of high-risk and high-return investments and low-risk and low return investments, and create a mixed portfolio that might be medium-high in return, and medium-low in risk. Your grandmother was right when she said to not put all your eggs in one basket.

PULLING IT ALL TOGETHER

Now let us tie together the concepts that we have gone over. An employee must make decisions about how much to save in their 403(b), as well as decide on an Asset Allocation arrangement. It seems clear that over long periods of time, investments in stocks seem to produce the highest investment results and give you the best chance of staying ahead of inflation. But you have to live with the market fluctuations. How much time you have until you use spend your money for retirement or another purpose is a crucial factor, as it lets you know how much time you have to ride out the ups and downs of the market.

Many financial planners use as a rule of thumb to estimate the **minimum percentage** of your retirement portfolio that you should invest in stocks that you should take your age and subtract it from 100. So a 35 year old would want to invest 65% *or more* of their retirement portfolio into stocks, while a 65 year old would only invest 35%. It may seem strange that a person who may be retired would still own a large amount of stocks, but a 65 year will live, on average, another 20 years. They still need to be concerned about the long-term effects of inflation.

Let us view three examples of how this concept of asset allocation might be put into practice.

EXAMPLES

Doctor A is 35 years old, married, and has recently purchased a home. Household income is $80,000 a year, but the mortgage and living expenses take up almost all of it. Doctor A elects to contribute only 5% of her salary into a 403(b) plan, knowing that she may contribute more heavily in future years to catch up. Because the time horizon for these investments is expected to be 25+ years, she elects to invest 75% of the money into a stock fund, and 25% into a high quality bond fund. She hopes the stocks provide a good, long-term return, while the presence of bonds in the portfolio will help reduce fluctuation.

Teacher B is 50 years old and married. Household income is $55,000. Knowing that his retirement is only 10 years or so away, Teacher B contributes 15% of his salary into a 403(b). He already has a large amount of non-403(b) investments, and will receive a pension and Social Security at age 62. He thinks he will not need money from the 403(b) for living expenses until he is 70 years or older (20 year time horizon). He already owns a large amount of American stock funds, but no amount of foreign stock funds, bond funds, or fixed annuities. He elects to divide the money 25% into a foreign stock fund, 25% into an American stock fund and 50% into a bond fund.

Professor C is 60 years old. Household income is $70,000. She plans to retire in 5 years, and is contributing 20% to maximize her 403(b) contributions in the last few years. She anticipates that she will start to use the 403(b) funds at retirement, along with a pension and Social Security. She is putting 40% into a stock fund, 20% into a fixed annuity, and 40% into a U.S. Government bond fund.

CONCLUSION

These are the four concepts about financial planning that you should always bear in mind. The first is the notion of risk and reward. There is no such thing as a "risk-free" investment. The second is the overwhelming importance of asset allocation and the benefits of diversification. It is the most important investment decision investors ever make. The third is how each investment category behaves in a general sense. The final one is simple, if you want more money when you retire, you need to save more now.

CHAPTER TEN

MOVING YOUR 403(b)s AROUND

Unlike most retirement plans, owners of 403(b)s have the right to switch their money around if they are dissatisfied with their current arrangement. This can be a very useful, particularly if your employer saddled you with some dud choices. Points to remember are:

* **HOW TO TRANSFER 403(b) FUNDS**

* **THE TAX CONSEQUENCES**

* **WHEN YOU WOULD MAKE THE CHANGE**

* **THE OTHER OPTION: IRA ROLLOVERS**

* **LOANS ON YOUR 403(b)**

* **TAKING PRE-RETIREMENT DISTRIBUTIONS**

Any investment is only as good as your ability to control it, and access the money. Additionally, the ability to "fire" the investment provider is a powerful tool to possess.

HOW TO MOVE 403(b) ASSETS AROUND

There is one major difference between the 403(b) plans and the 401(k) plans of which most people are unaware. This difference gives the 403(b) employee an enormous amount of control over his or her plan by allowing a greater freedom to move their money from one investment provider to another.

In a typical 401(k) plan, your employer chooses the choices you may use. If you are lucky, you will be given four to six different investment choices, all no-load (no sales charges). If you are not so lucky, you may get either one or two so-so investments, and/or have to pay sales charges when you invest. In either case, once you have taken advantage of the tax-deferral and placed funds in your 401(k) account, the money will generally remain within your company's set of choices until you leave the firm. You may be able to switch among these choices on some basis, perhaps quarterly or annually, but that is all.

In other words, if you decide that your set of choices are too expensive, or are not the type of investment you would like to make, you are stuck. You may not pull the money from those choices and take it somewhere else while you remain at your employer. As you may remember from earlier chapters, the money in a 401(k) is actually part of a trust fund controlled by the trustees. Your share of the money goes where they want it to go, even if they allow you some input into the matter.

There can be certain allowances for borrowing from your 401(k). There can also be certain provisions regarding withdrawing funds from your 401(k) prior to retirement or age 59 1/2 (see below). But neither of these methods makes much sense as a way to change investments.

The above is NOT true with most 403(b) arrangements. In most cases, the 403(b) arrangement is between the individual employee and the life insurance company or mutual fund family. Thanks to a ruling by the IRS (Revenue Ruling 90-24, 1990-1 CB 97), you may transfer 403(b) assets from one provider to another, without triggering taxes, and generally without the permission of your employer. This little known ruling gives you an enormous amount of control over your retirement funds.

WHEN WOULD YOU MAKE THE CHANGE?

The freedom to move your money is a valuable tool. There are several different situations where you might make use of this feature.

The first could occur if the choices you were offered were so limited that you could not make the types of investments that you felt were best for you. For example, if your employer only permitted one life insurance company to offer a fixed annuity as the sole option. An employee might decide that in the long run, the best investment for them might be a blue chip stock mutual fund. Perhaps they are fairly young, and feel that over twenty or more years, the stock fund is a much smarter option. They would want to move their funds out of the life insurance company and into a mutual fund 403(b) account. There is also the possibility that you are offered a small selection of mutual funds, but not the particular type or individual fund that you really want to invest in.

A second example would be if the fixed annuity choice was from a life insurance company that was offering noncompetitive interest rates. Or perhaps the company was undergoing financial difficulties, and you were concerned for its long-term financial health. In both cases, you might wish to keep using a fixed annuity, but switch to another life insurance company.

With variable annuities or mutual fund choices, you might decide that the expenses of your current offerings are much to high, and you would prefer to switch to a lower cost fund. Or perhaps the long term performance of the current offerings were poor compared to other funds of the same type.

If you were able to buy your current 403(b) investments without a sales load, or if you already paid a front-load on the money, you may move your existing funds without incurring any further charges from your current provider. But what if you have a back end-loaded mutual fund or an annuity with surrender charges? This is where you must make a difficult decision. The current provider will levy the surrender charges when you take your money out. On many annuities or mutual funds, this could cost you from 4% to 8% or more. If the funds have been in an account for a while, the charges might have dropped over the years to 1% or 2%, or even to 0%. The most recent additions to your 403(b) account may face higher charges. What should you do?

The first thing is to find out exactly how much, as a percentage of your current total, will you lose by switching the money. The investment provider should be able to provide you with an answer. Remember that older contributions may be charged a lower exit cost than newer contributions. With annuities, you may be able to withdraw some amount, such as 10% of the balance, without paying any surrender charge. The next thing is to estimate how much better your proposed new choice is compared to the old choice. For example, if you figure the new choice is 1% or 2% a year better, you can figure out how long it will take you to earn back the sales charge. If it is only a few years, it is may be worthwhile to switch now. In the example of a young employee whose only choice is a fixed annuity, they might earn as much as 4%-6% a year more, on average, by switching to a stock fund. If they have twenty years until retirement, they should make the switch, regardless of the surrender charge.

However, an investor should be wary if it is your broker or insurance agent who suggests making such a change. What they may see is the opportunity to make a second commission off of you. For example, let us say you that your broker or insurance agent has been collecting 5% as a sales commission on every dollar you put into your 403(b) annuity or mutual fund. If you stop putting money into your existing plan, they stop getting any commissions. But if you have accumulated $40,000 into this account, and they convince you to switch it to a "newer" and "better" annuity or mutual fund, they get a commission on the money a second time. On $40,000, the commission could be a $2,000. As we have discussed earlier, that money ultimately comes out of your pocket. In fact, the practice of selling an investor one annuity or fund, and then getting them to switch to a second choice just to generate another commission for the broker or agent, is against the law. In the brokerage business it is called "churning". In the life insurance industry it is called "twisting".

If you are going to change from your current option to a choice that you picked, it does not make much sense to turn around and pay another sales charge or get locked up with new surrender charges for another seven years. You should look around for a no-load choice whenever possible ("why pay for full service if you are going to pump your own gas?").

Often, investors stay in back end-load mutual funds and annuities because they don't want to pay the stiff surrender charge to change to another choice. But with most back end-loaded investments, you are going to be stuck for the cost whether you go and pay the surrender charge now, or stay and pay the higher annual expenses. Many people would chose to stay in an investment that is costing them an extra 1% a year in expenses for another 4 or 5 years, rather than pay a surrender charge today of 4% and move their funds. In fact, it is actually cheaper to get out now and pay 4%, than to stay and pay an extra 1% a year of an increasing account balance for the next 4 or 5 years.

THE TAX CONSEQUENCE

The transfer arrangement for 403(b)s is similar to the trustee-to-trustee transfer of money from one IRA account to another. As long as the funds do not pass through your hands, the transfer is considered a non-taxable event. This means that as long as the current life insurance company or mutual fund sends the money directly to the new life insurance company or mutual fund for another 403(b) account, you are in the clear from a tax standpoint.

Bear in mind that the above does NOT generally require the approval of your current employer. If you work for a hospital that gives you a choice on your 403(b) of one insurance company and one mutual fund family, your choices for contributions are limited to those options. But once you have funds in your 403(b) account, you may move it to another 403(b) account. There is one major exception to that rule. If your employer has also contributed money into your 403(b), you may not make the switch without their permission. However, as has been mentioned in the past, most employers do not contribute into employees' 403(b) accounts. If they do contribute funds for retirement, it is usually into a different retirement vehicle such as a pension plan.

As you can imagine, your current 403(b) plan provider is not keen on you knowing about this direct transfer option. Part of their reluctance is because they do not want to lose any assets. Part of their reluctance is because of some confusion about the rule establishing transfers. The ruling that permits them, Revenue Ruling 90-24, 1990-1 CB 97, does not explicitly state whether or not a life insurance company or mutual fund custodian account must include such an option in the 403(b) contracts. Other rulings seem to indicate that such an option will need to be included in future contracts. So as it stands right now, there are some life insurance companies, particularly those with older annuity contracts, that are not accepting instructions to transfer funds out to another 403(b).

The first thing you will need to do is read your annuity contract or 403(b) custodial agreement to see if it indicates if you may make such a transfer. Most newer policies will have such language in them. If it does not, contact the company and ask them their policy concerning transfers. You may find that you will have to ask a number of customer service people to find out the correct answer, so you may have to be persistent.

FINANCIALLY TROUBLED INSURANCE COMPANIES

A special tax rule applies in cases where you receive a cash distribution from your 403(b) annuity and the insurance company is in trouble. If the company is in conservatorship, rehabilitation, insolvency, or a similar state insurance commissioner proceeding, you may receive cash from the policy and place it back into a new 403(b), without triggering taxes. You must do so within 60 days of receive the cash, and you must include with your tax filings a statement that shows you made such a reinvestment.

MOVING FUNDS TO IRAs

There is another option that you have when you leave your employer. You can take the 403(b) funds and roll them over into an IRA. Generally, you may not do this as long as you are still employed by the hospital, school district, etc. But when you leave, you can make this choice. This is the same choice that an employee with a 401(k) is given. There are two methods that you may use.

In the first, you may do a **"direct rollover"** of the funds. Your current 403(b) investment provider will ask you for the name, address, and the account number of your IRA account. If you don't have one, you will need to set up an IRA account at the mutual fund, bank, brokerage firm, or insurance company that you plan to use. The 403(b) investment provider will then send the money directly to the IRA custodian. No funds are withheld for income taxes.

The other method is a cash distribution. The 403(b) provider will send YOU the check. However, if they do this, they must withhold 20% for income tax. You may still roll over the funds into an IRA, within 60 days, but you are missing the 20%. For example, if you have $20,000 in your 403(b) account, they will mail you $16,000. In order to avoid paying any taxes, you will need to place $20,000 into an IRA within sixty days. In other words, you will need to make up the missing $4,000 out of your own pocket. You will get the $4,000 back when you file your taxes. This means you may not see the money until April 15th of the following year. You have made Uncle Sam an interest-free loan of your money. As you can see, you will generally be better off doing a direct rollover.

LOANS FROM YOUR 403(b)

Under the Tax Code, it is permissible for a 403(b) account to offer a loan feature that would permit the employee to borrow funds from the investment provider, using their 403(b) balance as the collateral. If you receive cash under this method, it is NOT considered a distribution subject to income tax. There is no requirement that a 403(b) annuity or mutual fund 403(b) account offer this feature. However, many plans do offer this feature.

There is a limit to how much you may borrow from your 403(b). The limit is called the "50/50 rule". You may not borrow more than $50,000, or 50% of your balance, whichever is **less**. So if you had a balance of $70,000, your maximum loan amount could not exceed $35,000. There is one exception to the 50/50 rule. If your balance is less than $20,000, you may borrow up to $10,000 even if that figure exceeds 50%, although you may not borrow more than 100% of your balance.

The interest rate you will be charged on the funds must be a rate that is comparable to the rates on other secure loans prevailing at that time. For example, the life insurance company or mutual fund might set the interest rate based on the rate on home mortgages at the time the loan is made. You must make payments on the loan on at least a quarterly basis, and the payments should remain level over the life of the loan. The term of the loan cannot exceed 5 years. An exception exists if the loan is used to purchase a primary residence. In that case, loans may be payable over as many as 15 years. However, the interest paid on this loan is not tax-deductible. If you do not pay off your loan, the outstanding balance of the loan may be treated as a taxable distribution and reported to the IRS.

If you have a 403(b) plan that offers a loan feature, it gives you some additional financial flexibility. For example, if you needed a little extra cash to make the down payment on a house, or to take care of an unexpected emergency, you might tap into your 403(b). In that case, the feature is very beneficial. However, many employees may be tempted to use the balance to finance their lifestyle. For example, they may borrow money to pay for a vacation trip, intending to pay the money back later. There is a risk that an individual will find themselves spending their retirement funds for non-essential purchases, and than unable to pay the money back. As a general rule, an employee should only make use of the loan feature for an important reason and at a time when no other non-retirement financial assets are available to cover the cost.

TAKING PRE-RETIREMENT DISTRIBUTIONS

One of the trade-offs of almost all tax deferred arrangements is the requirement that you keep the funds in the plan until age 59 1/2. If you take money out before that time, you must pay income tax on the withdrawal and you will usually be charged a 10% penalty (there may also be a penalty from your State income tax agency). This penalty is to encourage people to use the funds for the purpose intended - retirement.

If you are over 59 1/2, the penalty does not apply, even if you are not yet retired.

There are several exceptions to the 10% penalty tax rule with 403(b) plans. The exceptions are similar to the exceptions for most other tax-deferred retirement plans. However, you must still claim the cash distributions as income and pay ordinary income tax on them. They include:

*   *Distributions made to the beneficiary at the death of the employee. So when you pass away, the funds are paid to your beneficiary and will be subject to income tax, but the 10% penalty will not apply. Please note that the first $5,000 paid under this method is generally not taxable.*

*   *Distributions made to an employee who has become disabled. If you become permanently disabled, you may take cash distributions and still avoid the 10% penalty.*

*   *Distributions made to a satisfy a "qualified domestic relations order" (QDRO). This is usually in the case of divorce. In these cases, the court will make a decision as to who gets what assets. The assets to be divided will include retirement plan balances.*

*   *Distributions made after the employee has left service AND is 55 years or older. So if you are no longer employed by your school district, hospital, college, or not-for-profit, and you have passed your 55th birthday, you may make withdrawals without triggering the 10% penalty.*

*   *Distributions that are made to employees who have certain levels of medical expenses The rules here are quite complicated and you will need to consult the IRS publications to determine if you meet these requirements.*

*   *Distributions made annually to the employee that are part of a series of substantially equal payments based on the life expectancies of the employee, or the employee and beneficiary. If you receive payments under this method, you must continue to receive the payments for at least 5 years, or until you turn 59 1/2, which ever is longer. For example, if you retire at 50, you can take out an amount each year from your 403(b) based on your life expectancy (the IRS has a life expectancy chart), as long as you keep receiving the payments until you reach 59 1/2. After that, you could stop the payments.*

As you can see, for many 403(b) investors, they will not have to wait until they are 59 1/2 to be able to start using the money without paying the 10% penalty. For example, if you retire early or have to stop working because of a medical condition, you can take advantage of one of the methods listed above. The 59 1/2 rule turns out to be much more flexible than many people think.

CHAPTER ELEVEN

WHEN YOUR ARE RETIRED

In the past chapters, most of what would apply to a person who owns a 403(b) account who is retired has already been covered. However, we will cover some areas of special concern. These areas include:

* WHAT DO I DO WITH THE MONEY NOW?

* SHOULD I ROLL THE FUNDS INTO AN IRA?

* CONVERTING TO AN IMMEDIATE ANNUITY

* WHEN MUST I BEGIN TO WITHDRAW FUNDS?

* WHAT HAPPENS IF I DIE WHILE STILL OWNING THE INVESTMENT?

* ESTATE TAX AND PROBATE CONCERNS

* CONCLUSION

For the prudent investor, this is where the payoff to the years of investing is realized. But there are still points to be aware of, and pitfalls to avoid.

WHAT SHOULD I DO NOW?

Congratulations! You are retired from your career AND you have an amount of money invested in a 403(b) plan. The question is "what to do now?".

The first thing you should do is make two promises to yourself. The first is not to allow yourself to be rushed into any decisions. The second promise is to not procrastinate too long about making any decisions.

When you retire, you may feel a need to hurry up and make some decisions about your money. At the same time, a number of investment sales types, with commissions in their eyes, will flock around you, each offering to help you with your money. Although some of them have good intentions, many of them view you and your nest egg as nothing more than a source of a large sales commission.

When you retire, the direction of your financial life usually changes. You will need time to sit down and think through what you should do now. Don't allow yourself to be rushed, there is plenty of time to make these decisions. If you retired when you were 65, the life expectancy charts say you will live, on average, another twenty years. A few months of thoughtful decision-making at this stage will not matter much.

On the other hand, you cannot put off the issue indefinitely. As the saying goes, "time is money". People have an enormous ability to put off critical thinking. You will come up with a million reasons why it will be better to wait until "next year" to look over your options. Let's be blunt, you are procrastinating! In most cases, your "reasons" to wait lack any real validity. A few months respite is okay, a year or more is not.

The starting point is to examine your entire financial worth and see how it corresponds to your needs and goals. The 403(b) funds are just part of the big picture. They, like IRA or other retirement plan funds, constitute the tax-deferred portion of your entire portfolio. You must examine all of the pieces of the puzzle. This is part of the financial planning process.

INCOME VERSUS GROWTH

In the pre-retirement stage of your investing, your primary goal was probably to have your 403(b) assets grow larger. You were very unlikely to need the money for current income. In fact, because of IRS penalties, you were largely prevented from using the investment for current income.

Now that you are retired, your situation MAY have changed. Depending on your current expenses and your other sources of income, you may need to draw money from your 403(b) as well. If this is the case, you will most likely tilt your 403(b)'s investment asset allocation towards income producing investments. For example, you might favor fixed annuities, bond mutual funds, or stock mutual funds that emphasize high dividend yielding stocks over a growth stock fund approach.

On the other hand, you may not need the income at this time. Between Social Security, pension payments, income from other investments, and income from a spouse, you may retire and currently not need any income from your 403(b) plan. In that case, you might tend to keep your investments tilted towards growth as they were before you retired, with a strategy of keeping your assets growing to combat inflation.

The first step to resolve this growth or income question is to look to your anticipated expenses. Add up your estimated expenses now that you are retired. Some expenses you may have to guess at, others you should know for certain.

Now add up all of the income that you will receive from non tax-deferred sources. Your Social Security and pension payments, interest and dividends from bank accounts, mutual funds, stocks, bonds, rents from real estate after expenses, and income from any business that you own. Do not, at this step, count earnings on your IRAs, 403(b)s, 401(k)s, or any other tax deferred investments that you own unless you are required to receive distributions (for example, if you are over 70 1/2). In that case, only count what you have to receive.

If you are already earning more than you are spending, there is no immediate need to add to your income by withdrawing from your tax-deferred plans. You might as well prolong the tax deferral for as long as possible. You will have to start receiving distributions when you turn 70 1/2, but for now you can remain in a growth mode.

EXAMPLE:
Ms. A retires at 65. She owns her own house, worth $120,000, and her expenses are $2,000 a month. She receives $1,500 a month from Social Security. She has $50,000 in the bank, $70,000 in a U.S. Government bond fund, and $75,000 in her 403(b). She currently has no problem. Her annual shortfall is $6,000, which she can cover from her non-tax deferred assets. She can leave the 403(b) to continue to grow until she is 70 1/2. Its' growth will be her main protection against inflation's effect on her expenses. Ms. A might leave her 403(b) portfolio in its' pre-retirement

110

asset allocation. For example, she may have had it invested 2/3 conservative stock fund, 1/3 U.S. Government bond fund. She has no compelling reason to change at this time.

If you do not receive enough income to cover your expenses, you actually have two options. First, you should examine your expenses in light of this new information. Even if you can cover your current expenses by withdrawing from your retirement plans, you may need to decide if you are spending too much money. You may need to depend on your financial resources for twenty or more years. You have to make sure that your spending patterns do not outstrip your long term resources. Now that you are retired, it is easy to spend money, but harder to make it.

EXAMPLE:
Mr. B retired at 62. He rents a house. He currently has $3,000 of monthly expenses. He earns $2,000 from Social Security and a pension. He has $50,000 in the bank, and $75,000 in his 403(b) plan. Mr. B. has a problem. His monthly shortfall is $12,000 a year. He only has a total of $125,000 of investment assets to produce that amount. Even if he could average 10% a year on his money, after taxes he would still not earn $12,000 a year. Remember that he pays taxes on the money he takes and spends from his 403(b). This means he will need to earn more than 10%, which is not easy, or dip into his principal. If he dips into his principal, eventually he will use up his money. Furthermore, he still needs some growth in his investments to offset inflation. He may need to cut back on his spending to insure that his resources will last. Because Mr. B's margin of safety is not very great, he might shift his portfolio from a pre-retirement asset allocation of 2/3 stock fund and 1/3 U.S. Government bond fund, to a more defensive 2/3 bonds and 1/3 stocks.

If you have adequate resources to support your long term spending habits, but need some of it to come from your retirement plans, you may restructure your retirement portfolio to produce more stable income, and give up some of the long-term growth potential. You can plan to draw on that income as you need it.

EXAMPLE:
Ms. C retired at 62. She owns her own house. She currently has expenses of $3,000 of monthly expenses. She receives $2,000 a month from Social Security and a pension. She has $50,000 in the bank, $75,000 in a U.S. Government bond mutual fund, and $150,000 in her 403(b). Ms. C does not have a problem. She needs $12,000 to cover her expense shortfall. She can easily get half of that from her taxable investments, and the rest from her 403(b). Even after taking some money from her 403(b), it

should still continue to grow. This is her protection against inflation in future years. Ms. C may switch her assets from her pre-retirement asset mix of 2/3 stock fund, 1/3 bond fund to a more balanced 1/2 of each.

SHOULD I ANNUITIZE?

When you have reached retirement age, you may receive an offer from your existing life insurance company or from an insurance agent suggesting that you "annuitize" your 403(b). What they are suggesting is that you convert your plan from a "deferred annuity" to an "immediate annuity". As you may recall from Chapter Six, an immediate annuity is one that pays you out a steady stream of payments over a period of time, usually over your lifetime. Also, your agent will usually get paid a commission if you annuitize.

Here is how it might work. Let us say that you retire and have $100,000 in your 403(b). Up to this time you have been letting it accumulate and grow. You now want to maximize your income. The life insurance company will offer to exchange with you your $100,000 for a monthly payment for the rest of your life. If you are 65 years of age, they might offer to pay you $687 a month ($8,244 a year), guaranteed by the life insurance company for the rest of your life. You may also accept a somewhat smaller monthly amount, but which will be paid out for the rest of your life and the life of your spouse. The question is, how good a deal is this for you?

The first concept to understand is that you are giving up the $100,000 for the payments. So when you die, there is nothing left to give your heirs. So your monthly payments are a mixture of interest and principal, and the payments stop when you, or perhaps your spouse, die. Once you start to receive the payments, you generally cannot back out of the deal. In the event of an emergency, you will not be able to retrieve your original balance. So you must be sure that the deal is a good one and that you have other resources to go to in the event of a problem. Obviously, if you intend to leave assets to your family, this option is a poor one.

The second concept to bear in mind is that the deal only makes sense for you if you live long enough. If you are 65 years of age, the calculations that the insurance company uses to come up with their monthly figure assume that you will live to be about 85. This is because the life expectancy of a 65 year old is about 20 years. But thelife insurance company pays you until you die. So if you live to be 95, you keep getting checks. From your standpoint, the deal looks pretty good. On the other hand, if you die at 75, it looks like a much worse deal for you. If you are in poor health or come from a family with a below average life expectancy, you may want to weigh carefully your options before going into this type of plan.

As far as the life insurance company is concerned, it all works out in the end. If they insure enough people, the law of averages say that for everyone that they have to pay for longer than expected, they will pay someone else for a shorter time period than expected.

However, aside from the problem of liquidity (you can't get at the principal once you accept the deal), and the risk of dying too early, you have one other major problem with accepting an immediate annuity. When you work out the numbers, you may get a very poor interest rate over time on your money. When the insurance company calculates the monthly payment your are going to be offered, they use three figures. The first is the balance to be invested. In our example, it is $100,000. The second figure they use is your life expectancy. For a 65 year old, it is about 20 years, or 240 months. The final figure is the "internal rate of return". This is the interest rate that thelife insurance company is figuring that they are paying you on the use of your money until you die.

Mathematically, the calculation works just like a 20-year home mortgage. The starting balance of the mortgage is $100,000. In 20 years (240 months) the balance will be zero. But how much your monthly mortgage payment is depends also on what interest rate you are charged. The higher the interest rate, the bigger your monthly payment. The lower the interest rate, the lower the monthly payment. An annuity calculation works exactly the same, except the life insurance company is making the payments to YOU.

How much your annuity will pay you each month depends not only on your age and the amount you originally invest, but also on the interest rate that the life insurance company uses in their calculation. However, unlike on your mortgage, thelife insurance company will not usually tell you what figure they used to calculate your monthly payment. Since you don't know the internal rate of return, you cannot judge if you are getting a good deal or not.

You could annuitize at a time when U.S. Government bonds are yielding 8%, but the life insurance company might only use 5% in their calculation. So they take your money, invest it spread out over twenty years in these bonds at 8%, and net 3% a year off you. Once you accept the deal, about $659 a month, you are locked in. At the same time, another life insurance company might be willing to offer an annuity using

5.5% as the internal rate of return. The monthly payment from that insurer would be higher, around $687 a month or almost $6,800 more in payments over twenty years. If you are going to annuitize, it pays to shop around.

As an alternative, you might take the same $100,000 and invest it in a U.S. Government bond fund that was yielding 8% at the time. You may also average 8% per year for the next 20 years. You could then turn around and systematically withdraw an amount every month based on your life expectancy. But since your own internal rate of return is 8%, not 5%, your monthly check would be higher than the life insurance company's monthly payment. In fact, if you did average 8%, your check would be $836 a month, or almost $43,000 more in total payments over 20 years compared to a 5% annuity.

There are a few differences between doing it yourself and using the annuity. The first is that if you do it yourself, it will be possible for your to spend all of the money while you are still alive. The life insurance company's annuity will normally continue to pay you for the rest of your life. On the other hand, if you die sooner than expected, your heirs would receive the unused balance of your bond fund. The annuity would leave them nothing. Also, in an emergency you could tap into the remaining principal of your own investment. A final difference is that with the life insurance company, you know that the internalrate of return will be 5%, unless the firm becomes insolvent. If you invest the money on your own through mutual funds, you may average more or less than 8%. On balance, the various factors tend to suggest that many people would be better off not annuitizing.

In order to do the calculations that will permit you to figure the internal rate of return, you should purchase a low cost calculator that does present and future values. Usually such a calculator will have preset buttons that will produce the results. So if you know 3 out of the 4 figures, you enter them in, and it will tell you the fourth figure. This is one way you can figure out for yourself what internal rate of return you are being offered by a life insurance company. You know how much you have to start with, what the monthly payment is that they are offering you, and your life expectancy based on your age (the IRS publishes a chart). You just need to have the calculator solve for the missing number, the interest rate.

403(b) VERSUS YOUR MORTGAGE

Another question that frequently comes up is whether a retired investor should use their tax-deferred funds, or any other funds for that matter, to pay off an outstanding balance on their home mortgage? The answer generally is no.

There are two reasons. First, you would have to pay taxes on what you withdraw from your 403(b). So if you have a $60,000 mortgage, you might need to withdraw $80,000-$90,000 from your 403(b) to pay it off. The second reason is simple. Paying off your mortgage early does not inherently make you any better off. You usually do not gain from the switch, and you frequently are worse off. Unsure as to why that is? You may approach the question from three different routes. You can consider it a question of assets, a question of income, or a choice of investments.

EXAMPLE:
Mr. D owns a house that is worth $150,000 at the present time. He owes $50,000 on the mortgage. His equity in the property is $100,000. He is paying 8% on the loan. He has $75,000 in his 403(b) and $75,000 in the bank. The $75,000 in the 403(b) is 1/2 a stock fund and 1/2 a U.S. Government bond fund. His total net worth is $250,000.

Assets: By liquidating part of his investments, Mr. D has essentially exchanged $50,000 of one asset, his 403(b) portfolio or his bank account, for $50,000 of another asset, more equity in his house. This produces no change to his overall level of wealth. He still has a net worth of $250,000.

Income: His mortgage costs him 8% That expense is tax deductible. After taxes, it may only cost him 5.5%. As long as he makes at least that much off his investments, after adjusting for taxes, he gains nothing by paying off the loan. In fact, it would not be difficult to earn 8%+ and have the earnings tax-deferred, as in his 403(b). The money in the bank may only be earning 5% taxable at the present time, but it also could be invested to earn more in another investment.

Investment Choice: Most people have seen the situation of someone who is "land rich and cash poor". Owning more real estate equity instead of other investments means that more of his portfolio will be tied up in less liquid investments. If he needs to turn assets into cash in a short amount of time, real estate is not a good choice of investments. Furthermore, he has a more unbalanced, less diversified portfolio. A larger percentage of his portfolio, 60%, would be tied up in real estate. If real estate goes up in value, he will not make money any faster because he paid off his house.

He will gain on the rise from the current $150,000, regardless of his loan. If real estate drops in value, he has fewer alternatives in his portfolio to cushion the blow. It is true that assets invested in stocks and bonds will fluctuate up and down, and the returns are unpredictable, but that is also true of real estate. If you think real estate only goes up, never down, ask someone in Southern California about the subject.

SHOULD I ROLL MY 403(b) INTO AN IRA?

You may transfer your 403(b) assets into an IRA after you have retired. Should you? As both types of plan are tax-deferred, there really is no tax advantage to making such a switch. If you are unhappy with your current 403(b) provider, you could switch to another 403(b) provider.

However, one advantage of the IRA transfer is that it would permit you to use investment choices besides mutual funds and insurance annuities. For example, you could invest into individual stocks and bonds, or into bank accounts using IRA accounts. This could prove useful if you wished to buy a portfolio of bonds with a range of maturity dates extending into the future. Such a portfolio is called a "laddered" portfolio. This could be particularly useful if you wish to self-annuitize your balance, as in the example earlier, instead of having a life insurance company provide you an annuity. However, unless you plan on making such a change in your investments, there is no reason to make the switch.

WHEN MUST I BEGIN TO WITHDRAW FUNDS?

The patience of the IRS and Uncle Sam is not endless when it comes to deferring taxes. Some day they want to tax your money. The day begins the year you turn 70 1/2 years of age.

Like most other tax-deferred plans, you must start withdrawing funds from your 403(b) and reporting as taxable income the proceeds for the tax year in which you turn 70 1/2. From that point on, you must withdraw a minimum amount each year. You may spend the money, invest it somewhere else, or give it away, but first you must claim it as income and pay any taxes that you may owe. There is an exception that may apply to you if you have a 403(b) plan with contributions from before 1987. In some cases, you may be able to delay making your mandatory, minimum distribution until you turn 75. You must be able to identify which are your pre-1987 funds.

The minimum withdrawal calculation is based on your life expectancy, or if you prefer, your life expectancy and the life expectancy of your

403(b) plan beneficiary.

EXAMPLE: *Ms. A turns 70 1/2 in August of this year. Based on the IRS chart, she has a life expectancy of 15. She must withdraw 1/15 of the dollar balance of her plan. The balance will be as of the end of last year, December 31. In the first year, she has up until April 1 of next year to make the withdrawal. For next year, and every other year after that, she must make the withdrawal by the end of the year. This means that if she waits until April 1 of next year for this year's distribution, she will have another distribution next year due by December 31.*

EXAMPLE: *Mr. B turns 70 1/2 years old in August. His beneficiary is Mrs. B, who is 70. According to the IRS chart, their combined life expectancy is 21 years. He must withdraw 1/21 by April 1 of next year.*

Because of the low percentage that must be withdrawn in the first few years, if you are earning 7% or 8% or more on your funds, the balance will actually still grow despite the withdrawals. However, each year, the life expectancy chart will go down, and the percentage that must be withdrawn will go up. Eventually, you are withdrawing money faster than it is growing, and your balance will begin to decline.

If you use a beneficiary who is NOT your spouse, for the purposes of calculating joint life expectancy they cannot be treated as being more than 10 years younger than you. This prevents people from using 3 year old grandchildren to stretch out the life expectancy tables.

If you own several different 403(b) accounts, you must calculate the minimum distribution required for each one. You may than withdraw that amount from one of the accounts, or a little bit from each. The choice is yours.

WHAT HAPPENS IF I DIE WHILE I STILL OWN THE PLAN?

When you die owning a 403(b), the money is paid by the life insurance company or mutual fund to your named beneficiary. If you do not name a beneficiary, the funds are owed to your estate. What happens to the money depends on your beneficiaries. If your beneficiary is your spouse, they may take all of the funds out and pay the taxes. They may also roll the funds into their own IRA account, thus continuing the tax-deferral.

If your beneficiary is not your spouse, they must take the money out. They can receive it all at once, or take it over a period of time. If they take it over a period of time, it matters if you were over 70 1/2 when you died. If you where not over 70 1/2, they can take the funds out in a lump sum within 5 years of your death, or in periodic payments based on their life expectancy, or faster. However, if you die after reaching 70 1/2, they must receive the periodic payments at least as fast as you, the original owner, would have received them.

ESTATE TAXES AND PROBATE CONCERNS

Your balances in your 403(b) plans will be counted as part of your estate for the purposes of calculating estate taxes. If your total estate exceeds $600,000, it may be subject to estate tax.

If you name a beneficiary, the money will pass to them without going through probate. Only if you do not designate a beneficiary will the funds be turned over to your estate. An important point here is that this means that the funds will go to your beneficiary regardless of what your will may state at that time. If you intend for the funds to go to someone other than the named beneficiary, you need to make a change in your account.

CONCLUSION

It was stated at the beginning of this book that the 403(b) plan was the"best retirement plan around". It was also stated that it was only true if the user knew how to make use of the features and benefits of this valuable retirement tool. After reviewing the material contained in this and the preceding chapters, hopefully the reader should feel confidant that they are a knowledgeable 403(b) user. In fact, the reader at this point most likely understands the 403(b) plan better then most employers, life insurance agents, and stockbrokers. The reader should understand how a 403(b) works, the role of their employer, how to select investment providers, and how a 403(b)fits into their retirement plans.

It is also hoped that the reader also feels, after reviewing the material, that the 403(b) is *"THE BEST RETIREMENT PLAN AROUND"*.

APPENDIX

IRS 403(b)

MAXIMUM CONTRIBUTION WORKSHEETS

Worksheet 1—Computation of Exclusion Allowance

Step 1—Exclusion Allowance

1) 20%   20%

2) Includible compensation for most
   recent one-year period of service $ _____

3) Years of service   _____

4) (1) × (2) × (3) $ _____

5) Minus: Amounts previously excludable
   (including prior year excess
   contributions)   _____

6) Exclusion allowance $ _____

Step 2—Amount Includible in Gross Income

7) Current year employer contributions
   (excluding cost of life insurance)* $ _____

8) Minus: Exclusion allowance (line 6)   _____

9) Amount includible in gross income $ _____

* The cost of life insurance is includible in gross income.

Worksheet 2—Limit on Employer Contributions

Step 1—Limit on Employer Contributions

1) Maximum ($30,000) or, if greater, ¼ of
   the dollar limit for defined benefit plans
   [See Limit on Employer Contributions.] $ _____

2) 25% of compensation $ _____

3) Limit on employer contributions [lesser
   of (1) or (2)] $ _____

Step 2—Contributions in Excess of Employer Limit

4) Current year contribution by employer
   (excluding term cost of life insurance)* $ _____

5) Minus: Limit on employer contributions
   (line 3)   _____

6) Excess (if any) $ _____

Step 3—Amount Excludable from Gross Income

7) a) Employer contribution (line 4) $ _____

   b) Limit on employer contributions (line
      3) $ _____

   c) Exclusion allowance (Worksheet 1,
      line 6) $ _____

8) Amount excludable from gross income
   [least of (a), (b), or (c)] $ _____

Step 4—Amount Includible in Gross Income

9) Employer contribution (line 4) $ _____

10) Minus: Amount excludable (line 8)   _____

11) Amount includible in gross income $ _____

* The cost of life insurance is includible in gross income.

Worksheet 3—Year of Separation from Service Limit Election [1]

Step 1—Limit on Employer Contributions

1) Maximum [See *Limit on Employer Contributions*.] $30,000

2) Exclusion allowance (modified)

   a) 20% 20%

   b) Includible compensation $ _____

   c) Years of service (limited to 10 years) _____

   d) (a) × (b) × (c) $ _____

   e) Minus: Amounts previously excludable during 10 years (including prior year excess contributions) _____

   f) Exclusion allowance (modified) $ _____

3) Limit on employer contributions [lesser of (1) or (2)(f)] $ _____

Step 2—Contributions in Excess of Employer Limit

4) Current year contribution by employer (excluding term cost of life insurance) [2] $ _____

5) Minus: Limit on employer contributions (line 3) _____

6) Excess (if any) $ _____

Step 3—Amount Excludable from Gross Income

7) a) Employer contribution (line 4) $ _____

   b) Limit on employer contributions (line 3) $ _____

   c) Exclusion allowance (Worksheet 1, line 6) $ _____

8) Amount excludable from gross income [least of (a), (b), or (c)] $ _____

Step 4—Amount Includible in Gross Income

9) Employer contribution $ _____

10) Minus: Amount excludable (line 8) $ _____

11) Amount includible in gross income $ _____

---

[1] Election applies only to employees of certain organizations. See *Special Election for Certain Employees*.
[2] The cost of life insurance is includible in gross income.

Worksheet 4—Any Year Limit Election [1]

Step 1—Limit on Employer Contributions
1) $4,000 plus 25% of includible compensation _____ $ _____

2) Exclusion allowance

   a) 20% _____ 20%

   b) Includible compensation $ _____

   c) Years of service _____

   d) (a) × (b) × (c) _____ $ _____

   e) Minus: Amounts previously excludable (including prior year excess contributions) _____

   f) Exclusion allowance _____ $ _____

3) Maximum _____ $ 15,000

4) Limit on employer contributions [least of (1), (2)(f), or (3)] _____ $ _____

Step 2—Contributions in Excess of Employer Limit
5) Current year contribution by employer (excluding term cost of life insurance) [2] _____ $ _____

6) Minus: Limit on employer contributions (line 4) _____

7) Excess (if any) _____ $ _____

Step 3—Amount Excludable from Gross Income
8) a) Employer contribution (line 5) _____ $ _____

   b) Limit on employer contributions (line 4) $ _____

   c) Exclusion allowance (Worksheet 1, line 6) $ _____

9) Amount excludable from gross income [least of (a), (b), or (c)] _____ $ _____

Step 4—Amount Includible in Gross Income
10) Employer contribution (line 5) _____ $ _____

11) Minus: Amount excludable (line 9) _____

12) Amount includible in gross income _____ $ _____

[1] Election applies only to employees of certain organizations. See *Special Election for Certain Employees.*
[2] The cost of life insurance is includible in gross income.

Worksheet 5—Overall Limit Election [1,2]

Step 1—Limit on Employer Contributions
1) Maximum [See *Limit on Employer Contributions*] $ 30,000

2) 25% × compensation [See *Compensation*, earlier, under *Limit on Employer Contributions*.] $ _____

3) Limit on employer contributions [lesser of (1) or (2)] $ _____

Step 2—Contributions in Excess of Employer Limitation
4) Current year contribution by employer (excluding term cost of life insurance)[3] $ _____

5) Minus: Limit on employer contributions (line 3)   _____

6) Excess (if any) $ _____

Step 3—Amount Excludable from Gross Income
7) a) Employer contribution (line 4) $ _____

   b) Limit on employer contributions (line 3) $ _____

8) Amount excludable from gross income [lesser of (a) or (b)] $ _____

Step 4—Amount Includible in Gross Income
9) Employer contribution (line 4) $ _____

10) Minus: Amount excludable (line 8)   _____

11) Amount includible in gross income $ _____

[1] Election applies only to employees of certain organizations. See *Special Election for Certain Employees.*
[2] Limit on employer contributions is considered equal to the exclusion allowance.
[3] The cost of life insurance is includible in gross income.

Worksheet 6—Limit on Elective Deferrals

Step 1—Total Elective Deferrals

1) Contributions to tax-sheltered annuities $ _____

2) Contributions to cash or deferred arrangements (section 401(k) plans) or section 501(c)(18) plans   _____

3) Elective contributions to salary reduction simplified employee pension (SEP) plans   _____

4) Total deferrals for year (add lines (1), (2), and (3)) $ _____

Step 2—Increase in Limit for Long Service

Note: Skip this step if you do not have at least 15 years service with a qualifying organization (see *Special Election for Certain Employees,* earlier).

5) Number of years service with the qualifying organization   _____

6) Multiply $5,000 by the number of years in (5) $ _____

7) Total elective deferrals for prior years made for you by the qualifying organization   _____

8) Subtract line (7) from line (6) $ _____

9) Enter all increases in the limit for long service (as figured in this Step 2) for prior years $ _____

10) Subtract line (9) from $15,000 $ _____

11) Enter the smaller of line (8) or line (10), but not more than $3,000 $ _____

Step 3—Limit on Elective Deferrals

12) Enter $9,500 plus the amount from line (11) $ _____

13) Basic allowable amount (enter $9,240 for 1994)   _____

14) Subtract line (13) from line (12)   _____

15) Enter the smaller of line (1) or line (14)   _____

16) Add lines (13) and (15). This is your limit on elective deferrals for the year $ _____

17) Excess elective deferrals—Subtract line (16) from line (4). Do not enter less than zero. Include this amount in your income for the year the excess deferrals were made, unless you withdraw it by April 15 of the following year. $ _____

ABOUT THE AUTHOR

John T. Hyland is a manager of retirement plan services at a mutual
fund company based in San Francisco, California. He is responsible
for retirement plan design and administration, as well as investment
management. In his professional career, he has been a bank officer,
a stock broker, and a life insurance agent. He is a graduate of the
University of California, Berkeley. He also holds the designation of
Chartered Financial Analysts (CFA), and sits on the Board of
Directors of the Securities Analysts of San Francisco Society.